Indonesian
phrasebook

**Paul Woods
Kristiana Sarwao Rini
Margit Meinhold**

S0-AEL-575

Indonesian Phrasebook
   3rd edition

Published by
   Lonely Planet Publications
   Head Office: PO Box 617, Hawthorn, Vic 3122, Australia
   Branches: 155 Filbert Street, Suite 251, Oakland CA 94607, USA
                10 Barley Mow Passage, Chiswick, London W4 4PH, UK
                71 bis rue de Cardinal Lemoine, 75005 Paris, France

Printed by
   Colorcraft Ltd, Hong Kong
   Printed in China

Cover photograph
   Wooden Balinese carving, detail (Tamsin Wilson)

Published
   July 1995

About This Book

This edition was updated by Tina Gultom. The 2nd edition was written by
Paul Woods and Kristiana Sarwo Rini, and the 1st edition was written by Margit
Meinhold. Sally Steward edited the book, Tamsin Wilson was responsible for
the cover and illustrations, and Penelope Richardson for design.

National Library of Australia Cataloguing in Publication Data

Woods, Paul
   Indonesian Phrasebook
   3rd ed.
   ISBN 0 86442 342 X

   1. Indonesian language – Conversation and phrase books – English. I.
   Meinhold, Margit. Indonesia phrasebook. II. Title. (Series: Language
   survival kit).

499.22183421
© Copyright Lonely Planet 1995

All rights reserved. No part of this publication may be reproduced, stored in a
retrieval system or transmitted in any form by any means, electronic, mechan-
ical, photocopying, recording or otherwise, except brief extracts for the
purpose of review, without the written permission of the publisher and copyright owner.

Contents

Introduction

Indonesian, or Bahasa Indonesia as it is more correctly called, is the lingua franca of Indonesia. It was first used formally by nationalists Sukarno and Mohammed Hatta to write the declaration of Indonesian independence in August 1945. The language was a symbol of unity and nationalism at that time, and was later adopted as the national language of education and government throughout Indonesia. There are, however, over 300 different languages spoken throughout Indonesia, so you'll find most people use their own local language, *bahasa daerah*, at home and Bahasa Indonesia to communicate with visitors. Most people you meet in Indonesia (with the exception of Irian Jaya) will speak Bahasa Indonesia well – it is usually only the older people and preschool children who are not fluent. Jakarta, as the melting pot of Indonesia, has even developed its own characteristic dialect, called *Bahasa Betawi*, from the old Dutch name for the capital of the Dutch East Indies, 'Batavia'.

Bahasa Indonesia is derived from Malay, which was used for many centuries as the language of traders who plied the Indonesian archipeligo. These included Arabs, Chinese, Portuguese and Dutch, whose languages have all left their legacy in today's Bahasa Indonesia. It is a very dynamic language and is constantly absorbing new vocabulary, more recent influences including English, which is now the most popular foreign language.

One of the best aspects of travelling in Indonesia and learning Indonesian is that even your most stumbling attempts in the language will be greeted with enthusiasm. Just a few words spoken will be rewarded with the exclamation *'Wah, sudah lancar bahasa Indonesianya'*, which is a compliment on your fluency.

6 Help!

What is important and appreciated is your attempt, rather than your ability. This has got to be one of the reasons why so many people pick up a reasonable ability to communicate in only a few weeks' stay in Indonesia, and get a great deal of enjoyment in the process.

Bahasa Indonesia (literally 'language of Indonesia') is an easy language to pick up for the purpose of everyday communication. There are, however, a few points to note. To be able to read and write Bahasa Indonesia well takes a long period of study, just like any other language, because of the use of complex grammar which is not used in everyday speech, and the fact that formal writings contain a far greater range of vocabulary than is used in speaking. So don't expect to be able to read the newspaper after one month in Indonesia.

Everyday speech is a very simplified form of the language, which is a great plus for beginners, however you'll find that people communicate with each other at such a machinegun speed that you'll be left well behind. This is why you'll need to master *'Ma'af, Bahasa Indonesia saya belum lancar'* (pronounced 'lanchar'), which means 'I'm not yet fluent in Indonesian', in order to avoid being overwhelmed by a burst of local dialect.

This phrasebook has been designed to enable you to travel independently in Indonesia. It is an invaluable companion to the comprehensive guidebook, *Indonesia: a travel survival kit*, also published by Lonely Planet.

Selamat jalan! – Bon voyage!

Help!

It's not hard to memorise the key words you'll need for your trip. *Tolong* and *ma'af*, Please, *Terimah kasih* (pronounced 'ka-see') Thank you and *Kembali*, 'You're welcome.' You'll be hearing these all the time. Yes is *Ya* and No is *Tidak*. How much? is *Berapa ongkosnya*?

If you're having trouble understanding or being understood, see page 35 for help.

Selamat (pronounced 'sla-mat') *siang* is Good day, *Selamat sore* (pronounced 'so-ray') is Good afternoon. For more on greetings, see page 25.

To indicate time, there are three words you can use: *sedang*, for something that is happening now; *sudah*, to indicate the past; and *akan*, the future. See pages 16 to 17 for more on this, and the Vocabulary chapter for key words.

Pronunciation

Indonesian is an easy language to learn, and even easier to pronounce as it is a phonetic language, with each single letter representing one sound. With a couple of exceptions, the sounds are the same every time and receive equal emphasis. Generally, the second-to-last syllable in a word is stressed, and in sentences, stress is on the most important word.

Vowels

a like the 'u' in 'hut' or 'up'

Apa kabar?		How are you?
Kabar baik.		Fine thanks.

e a short sound, like the 'e' in 'earn', when it is unstressed, in which case it is hardly pronounced at all, or like the 'e' in 'café' when it is stressed. A stressed **e** at the end of a word is a little longer, but the stress can also fall on other syllables.

Selamat sore.	'slamat **so**ray'	Good afternoon.
meja	'**may**-ja'	table
merdeka	'mer-**day**-ka'	free

i like the 'i' in 'unique'. The length of the sound doesn't alter.

Selamat tidur.	'slamat tee-dur'	Good night.
Selamat tinggal.	'slamat ting gal'	Farewell.

o similar to the English 'o' sound in either 'hot' or 'cold'. Generally speaking you won't be misunderstood if you pronounce this sound as you would in English.

foto		photograph
obat		medicine

u   as the 'oo' in 'too', only shorter

satu   'satoo'   one

Diphthongs

There are also three vowel combinations: **ai**, **au** and **ua**. The first
two sounds are true diphthongs, the **ua** a combination of sounds.

ai   sounds like 'i' in 'like'

Kabar baik.   'kabar bai'   I'm fine.

au   sounds like a drawn out 'ow' like 'cow'

saudara   'sowdara'   you (or brother)
mau   as in Chairman   want
                   'Mao'

PRONUNCIATION

ua begins with the sound of 'oo' as in 'too' and ends with the 'ah' sound in 'hut', with a glide, like a slight 'w' sound, sounded between the letters.

| *uang* | 'oowahng' | money |
| *puas* | 'poowahs' | satisfied |

Consonants

The pronunciation of consonants is very straightforward. Each is pronounced consistently, and most sound like English.

b as the 'b' in 'better' at the beginning or middle of a word; as the 'b' in 'rub' (almost a 'p' sound) at the end of a word

| *bagi* | 'ba-gee' | for |
| *lembab* | 'lem-babp' | humid |

p as the 'p' in 'lip'

| *panas* | 'pa-nas' | hot |

c 'ch' as in 'chair'

| *karcis* | 'kar-chis' | ticket |

g   always pronounced hard, as the 'g' in 'garden'
    pagi   'pa-gee'   morning

ng   always pronounced as the 'ng' in 'sing'
    siang   'si-yang'   day
    tinggal   'ting-gal'   live

j   pronounced as 'dj'. It's the sound you hear at the beginning
of 'join'.
    tujuh   'tud-juh'   seven

r   pronounced very clearly and distinctly. It is always slightly
trilled.
    Apa kabar?   'apa ka-barrr'   How are you?
    Selamat tidur. 'slamat tee-durrr' Good night.

h   always pronounced. It is stressed a little more strongly than in English, as if you were sighing. This heavy pronunciation is particularly true for words of Arabic origin, when the 'h' appears between two vowels which are the same.

hotel	'hhotel'	hotel
mahal	'mahhhal'	expensive
Rupiah	'rupiahh'	local currency

k   pronounced the same as the English 'k', unless it appears at the end of a word, when you should soften it, stopping just short of actually saying the 'k'.

Kabar baik.	'ka-bar bai'	I'm well.

ny   a single sound, like the 'ny' in 'canyon' or the beginning of 'new', before the 'oo' part of the word.

nyonya	'nyo-nya'	Mrs

Grammar

Indonesian grammar is simple to master for the purpose of basic communication. Nouns do not have plural forms, the pattern of sentences is straightforward, and sentences are usually short.

Word Order

The word order for Indonesian sentences is the same as for English sentences: subject, verb, object. The simplest sentence structure of 'subject, verb, object' can be illustrated with *Saya membaca buku*, literally 'I reading book': 'I am reading a book'.

It is quite common in Indonesian for the object to be mentioned first. This however requires modification of the verb form and so it is easier as a beginner in Indonesian to simply use the subject-verb-object construction illustrated above.

There are no special terms for 'is' and 'are'. Thus *Buku merah*, literally 'book red', means 'The book is red'. The articles, 'a' and 'the' are either implied by the noun or indicated by the word *yang*. So to say 'The red book' you will say *Buku yang merah*.

For sentences where no subject is obvious, the word *ada* is used. *Ada* is the nearest equivalent to 'there is', but means 'to be' in the sense of 'to exist'. *Ada buku yang merah*, for example, means 'There is a red book'. It may also be used to indicate possession, for example *Saya ada uang*, which means 'I have money' (literally: 'there is money on me').

Verbs

Indonesian has a basic verb form which may be used in colloquial speech, and you will be understood perfectly well when you use

13

GRAMMAR

it. You will notice however, that in more formal situations and for use in written communication, there is a system of prefixes and suffixes which are added to the root word. The correct prefix or suffix depends on the type of verb and its context in the sentence.

Types of Verbs
There are basically three types or classes of verbs.

- The simplest type stands alone and never requires a prefix, when used as a verb. Fortunately many of the most commonly used verbs fit into this category:

to sit	*duduk*
to eat	*makan*
to drink	*minum*
to cook	*masak*
to bathe	*mandi*
to go	*pergi*

- The second category is the 'ber verbs', because *ber* is used as a prefix to the root word. For example, the root word *bicara* becomes *berbicara,* 'to speak'. If the root word starts with 'r', such as *renang*, 'to swim', the prefix drops the 'r' and becomes *be*: *berenang*.

  'Ber verbs' are quite common:

to ask	*bertanya*
to play	*bermain*
to run	*berlari*
to swim	*berenang*

- The third category is verbs which use the *me* prefix. Note that the prefix varies a little from word to word, and the root word is sometimes modified, so that, for instance, the root word for 'read', *tulis*, becomes *menulis*:

to read	*membaca*
to write	*menulis*
to answer	*menjawab*
to buy	*membeli*
to open	*membuka*
to search	*mencari*
to assist	*membantu*

The correct use of prefixes with verbs takes a long time to master, and there are other forms of verbs as well as those mentioned here, but remember that in everyday speech the use of the root word alone will nevertheless convey a clear meaning.

GRAMMAR

GRAMMAR

Tense

Verbs do not change their form with tense. Tense can be denoted by context, such as the insertion of a time word such as *besok*, 'tomorrow', and *kemarin*, 'yesterday', at the beginning of a sentence. For example *Kemarin saya membeli mobil* means 'I bought a car yesterday', while *Besok saya mau membeli mobil* means 'I will buy a car tomorrow'.

Alternatively, there are several special tense indicators which are always placed immediately before the verb in a sentence. The most common are *sudah*, *sedang* and *akan* which denote past, present and future tenses, respectively. For example *Saya sudah makan* means 'I have already eaten', *Saya sedang makan* means 'I'm still eating' and *Saya akan makan*, meaning 'I will eat', shows that the action is in the future. For an action which has very recently taken place we can use *baru saja*: *Saya baru saja makan* 'I have just finished eating'.

To illustrate sentence construction and the use of verbs, here are a few examples:

to eat	*makan*
The man eats chicken.	*Orang itu makan ayam.*
to drink	*minum*
I want to drink tea.	*Saya mau minum teh.*
to want	*mau*
They want to sleep.	*Mereka mau tidur.*
to go	*pergi*
The children go to the shop.	*Anak-anak pergi ke toko.*

Adjectives

Adjectives follow the noun:

red book	*buku merah*
this book	*buku ini*
my book	*buku saya*
big house	*rumah besar*

When you want to say more than one thing about the noun you use '... *yang* ...':

the small red book	*buku merah yang kecil*
	'book red which [is] small'
the big white house	*rumah putih yang besar*
	'house white which [is] big'

Comparisons in Indonesian are made with the use of *lebih*, 'more' and *kurang*, 'less' – both placed before the adjective. *Daripada* is also used in the place of 'than' in English, if both objects being compared are specifically mentioned. For example *Mangga lebih mahal daripada pisang*, 'Mangoes are more expensive than bananas'.

bigger than	*lebih besar daripada*
	'more big than'
smaller than	*lebih kecil daripada*
	'more small than'
more delicious than	*lebih enak daripada*
fewer than	*lebih sedikit daripada*
more than	*lebih banyak daripada*

To indicate extremes of comparison, *yang paling* is used:

the biggest shop	*toko yang paling besar*
the smallest shop	*toko yang paling kecil*
cheapest	*yang paling murah*
This car is the cheapest.	*Mobil ini yang paling murah.*
the most expensive	*yang paling mahal*
That hotel is the most expensive.	*Hotel itu yang paling mahal.*

Pronouns
Personal Pronouns

Personal pronouns reflect levels of politeness. When addressing someone, you can use *Bapak* (literally: 'father') and *Ibu* (literally: 'mother'), which are commonly used respectful terms for an older man or woman, instead of one of the 'you' forms. You won't be wrong if you use *Bapak* or *Ibu* to address someone, unless they are very young.

There are three forms of the words 'you'. *Saudara*, (literally: 'relative'), is the most formal version and it's acceptable in most situations. *Kamu* is used only with friends and among young people. The word *anda* also means 'you' and may be heard in everyday speech.

The first person plural, 'we', has two different words in Indonesian: *kita*, 'we', when including the person spoken to; and *kami*, which only includes the people spoken about and not the person being addressed.

Let's go to lunch.	*Mari kita pergi makan siang.*
We're going to lunch (but you're not).	*Kami akan pergi makan siang.*

I/my	*saya*
you (sg)	*saudara/kamu/anda*
he/she	*ia/dia*
we	*kami/kita*
you (pl)	*saudara sekalian*/kalian*
they	*mereka*

* *Saudara sekalian* is more formal than *kalian*.

Possessive Pronouns

The first and second possessive pronouns ('my' and 'your') and the third person plural ('their') are the same as the personal pronouns and are placed after the noun.

my jacket	*jaket saya*
your ticket	*karcis saudara*
their house	*rumah mereka*

The way to indicate possession in the third person (he, she or they), is to use the suffix *nya* with the verb:

his jacket	*jaketnya*
his/her money	*uangnya*

Questions

The structure of question sentences is not difficult to master. You can make a question by simply raising the pitch of your voice at the end of the sentence.

There are a number of question words you may want to use as well. These are put at the beginning of the sentence:

what	*apa*
How are you?	*Apa kabar?*
who	*siapa*
What is your name?	*Siapa nama saudara?*
when	*kapan*
When does the bus leave?	*Kapan bisnya berangkat?*
where	*dimana*
Where is the station?	*Dimana stasiun?*
from where	*darimana*
Where have you been?	*Darimana?*
to where	*kemana*
Where does the bus go to?	*Kemana bisnya pergi?*
how/in what way	*bagaimana*
What's the hotel like?	*Bagaimana hotelnya?*
how much/many	*berapa*
How much is this?	*Berapa harganya ini?*
How many people?	*Berapa orang?*
why	*mengapa*
Why is the bus late?	*Mengapa bisnya terlambat?*

GRAMMAR

| may I? | boleh? |
| May I come in? | Boleh saya masuk? |

A third possible way to make a question is by the addition of *kah* to the end of the most important word, that is, the word the question is about. You may wish to make use of this when you have acquired a certain level of proficiency. You can certainly get by without it.

Negation

Tidak, *bukan* and *jangan* are used to indicate negation. *Tidak* and *jangan* are put in front of verbs and adjectives, while *bukan* is put in front of nouns:

I don't want to.	Saya tidak mau.
That's not it.	Bukan yang itu.
Don't run.	Jangan lari.

Both *tidak* and *bukan* can be used on their own to mean 'No' in answer to a question.

Do you like bread?	Suka roti?
No (I don't).	Tidak.
This one?	Yang ini?
No (not this one).	Bukan.

Plurals

The same word is used for singular or plural. There are no endings in Indonesian which may be attached to a word to make it plural. Generally the context will indicate whether something is plural or not. For example *banyak orang* means 'many people'. In writing, the noun is repeated to indicate plural:

child	*anak*
children	*anak-anak*

Doubling a word has several other functions. It can sometimes intensify the actual meaning of the word.

slow	*pelan*
slowly	*pelan-pelan*
sit	*duduk*
sitting around	*duduk-duduk*

Because of this potential for confusion it's probably best to avoid indiscriminate doubling. Quantity can be indicated by a number, or a quantity word placed before the noun.

Quantity Words

all	*semua*
both	*keduanya/dua-duanya*
each	*tiap-tiap/setiap*
enough	*cukup*
every/each	*masing-masing*
little	*sedikit*
many/much	*banyak*
some/few	*beberapa*

These quantity words always precede the noun they qualify:

There are many people.	*Ada banyak orang.*

Adverbs

always	*selalu*
also	*juga*
immediately	*dengan segera/secepatnya*
never	*tidak pernah*
not yet	*belum*
often	*sering*
perhaps	*barangkali/bisa jadi*
possibly	*mungkin*
really	*sungguh*
too (also)	*juga*
too [big, small, etc]	*terlalu*
very (quite)	*sekali*

GRAMMAR

Comparisons

Comparisons that in English would be indicated by 'as ... as' are indicated in Indonesian by the prefix *se*:

as big as	*sebesar*
as soon as	*secepat*
as wide as	*selebar*
as white as	*seputih*

Conjunctions

after	*sesudah*
as big as	*sebesar*
as soon as	*secepat*
because	*karena/sebab*
before	*sebelum*
if	*kalau*
or	*atau*

since	*sejak*
when	*waktu*
while	*sedang/sementara*

Prepositions

about	*tentang/mengenai*
at, in, on (place)	*di*
at, in (time)	*jam, dalam*
between	*antara*
during	*selama*
for	*untuk*
from	*dari*
on	*pada*
since	*sejak*
through	*melalui*
till	*sampai*
to	*ke*
with	*dengan*
without	*tanpa*

Greetings & Civilities

People in Indonesia put more emphasis on politeness and civilities than you may be accustomed to, so you will be accepted much better if you use the common civilities.

Greetings

In English we can say 'Good morning' or 'Good evening' or 'Good day', depending on the time of day. It's the same in Indonesian.

Good morning. (5 – 11 am)	*Selamat pagi.*
Good day. (11 am – 3 pm)	*Selamat siang.*
Good afternoon. (3 – 7 pm)	*Selamat sore.*
Good evening. (after dark)	*Selamat malam.*
Good night. (on retiring)	*Selamat tidur.*

Civilities

For many Indonesians it is a sign of polite restraint not to accept an offer when it is first made. Therefore, if you are offering somebody something don't be deterred by their first refusal. Repeat the offer and it will probably be accepted.

When you are visiting somebody in their house you may be served a sweet drink which is considered better than offering coffee or tea, and is sometimes accompanied by a snack. If it is not to your liking, it is quite acceptable to take just a few sips. If you don't want to take the snack, just say *Ma'af, saya masih kenyang*, ('Sorry, I'm still full') or *Ma'af, saya baru makan*, (Sorry, I've just eaten).

Enjoy your meal.	*Selamat makan.*
Enjoy your drink.	*Selamat minum.*
Farewell.	*Selamat tinggal.*
(when you are leaving)	
Farewell.	*Selamat jalan.*
(when others are leaving but you are staying)	
Goodnight.	*Selamat tidur.*
Welcome.	*Selamat datang.*
See you later.	*Sampai jumpa lagi.*

Selamat, which means 'May your action be blessed', comes from the Arabic word, *salam*. Putting this word together with 'morning' or 'evening' then translates into something like 'Have a nice morning/evening'. All sorts of actions may be blessed, and *selamat* is a word you will hear quite often.

In Indonesian there are two words for 'please'. *Tolong* is used when you are making a request or when you are asking somebody to do something for you. If you are offering something to somebody you use *silakan*. For example:

please/help	*tolong*
Please shut the door.	*Tolong tutup pintu itu.*
Please clean my room.	*Tolong bersihkan kamar saya.*
Please come in.	*Silakan masuk.*
Please sit down.	*Silakan duduk.*

Although people appreciate politeness, you will find that 'thank you' is used less frequently than in English.

Thank you.	*Terima kasih.*
You're welcome.	*Kembali.*
You're welcome. (colloquial)	*Sama-sama.*
Excuse me.	*Permisi.*
Pardon? (What did you say?)	*Ma'af?*
I'm sorry ... (apology)	*Ma'af ...*

Forms of Address

In Indonesia you will hear various forms of address. The most usual is the *Ibu/Bapak* combination. These words literally mean 'Mother' and 'Father'. They are also used in situations which require a greater show of respect or a greater degree of formality, as in a passport office, for instance. *Saudara* literally means 'brother' or 'sister' and it can be used to mean 'you', which shows a degree of respect. When talking to children you may want to use *kamu* or *dik*, from the word *adik*, meaning younger brother or sister.

Mr	*Bapak, Pak*
Mrs	*Ibu*
Miss	*Nona*

Body Language

Shaking hands in Indonesia involves only a light brief touch of the hand, and is suitable for both men and women. It is appropriate to shake hands when being introduced to somebody, when visiting somebody in their house, or when you haven't seen somebody for a while.

GREETINGS

It is considered polite to bow your body slightly when walking across in front of somebody who is seated or if interrupting people. At the same time you can say *permisi*, which just means 'excuse me'.

Standing with your hands on your hips is considered rude and therefore should be avoided. When sitting, tuck your feet away so they aren't pointing towards people. Don't touch people on the head, and don't point with your forefinger.

Small Talk

As you travel around Indonesia you will be meeting people and wanting to make conversation. You will almost certainly be asked questions about yourself and the members of your family.

Meeting People

What is your name?	*Siapa nama saudara?*
My name is ...	*Nama saya ...*

Nationalities

Where are you from?	*Dari mana asal saudara?*
I am from ...	*Saya dari ...*
Australia	*Australia*
Canada	*Kanada*
England	*Inggris*
Europe	*Eropa*
Ireland	*Irlandia*
Japan	*Jepang*
New Zealand	*Selandia Baru*
Scotland	*Skotlandia*
the USA	*Amerika*

I am a/an...	*Saya ...*
Australian	*orang Australia*
American	*orang Amerika*
British	*orang Inggris*
Canadian	*orang Kanada*
Dutch	*orang Belanda*

English	*orang Inggris*
foreigner	*orang asing*
Irish	*orang Irlandia*
New Zealander	*orang Selandia Baru*

Age

How old are you?	*Berapa umur saudara?*
I am …	*Umur saya …*
20 years old	*duapuluh tahun*
35 years old	*tigapuluh lima tahun*

Occupations

What is your occupation?	*Apa pekerjaan saudara?*
(I am a/an …)	
artist	*seniman*
businessperson	*pengusaha*
doctor	*dokter*
engineer	*insinyur*
factory worker	*pekerja pabrik*
farmer	*petani*
journalist	*wartawan*
lawyer	*ahli hukum*
mechanic	*montir*
musician	*pemain musik*
nurse	*perawat*
public servant	*pegawai negeri*
sailor	*pelaut*
singer	*penyanyi*
scientist	*ahli sains*
secretary	*sekretaris*
student (school)	*pelajar*
student (university)	*mahasiswa*
teacher	*guru*
writer	*penulis*

Religion

What is your religion?	*Apa agama saudara?*
My religion is …	*Agama saya …*
Buddhist	*Budha*
Catholic	*Katolik*
Christian	*Kristen*

SMALL TALK

Hindu	*Hindu*
Jewish	*Yahudi*
Muslim	*Islam*

Most Indonesians are Muslim, some are Christian, a few are Hindu and Buddhist. Indonesians may feel uncomfortable if you do not profess a religion, often equating atheism with communism. Therefore, you will maintain better relations by claiming to have a religion.

Family

This is my ...	*Ini ... saya*
mother	*ibu*
father	*bapak*
older sister/brother	*kakak perempuan/laki-laki*
younger sister/brother	*adik perempuan/laki-laki*
child	*anak*
children	*anak-anak*
son	*anak laki-laki*
daughter	*anak perempuan*
husband	*suami*
wife	*istri*
friend	*teman*
boyfriend/girlfriend	*pacar*
partner	*pasangan*

Questions about you and your life will be asked quite frequently, in particular, *Sudah kawin?*, 'Are you already married?'. Unless you are indeed married, the appropriate answer is *Belum!*, 'Not yet!'

Tidak, 'No', would be grammatically fine to use, but most

Indonesians would not understand why you should not be married or not thinking about it. You will get on a lot better, especially if you are a woman, if you answer *Sudah* or *Belum*.

already	*sudah*
not yet	*belum*
no	*tidak*

Are you married?	*Sudah nikah/kawin?*
I am not married yet.	*Saya belum nikah/kawin.*
I am married.	*Saya sudah nikah/kawin.*

Do you have any children?	Punya anak?
I don't have any children.	Saya tidak punya anak.
I don't have any children yet.	Saya belum punya anak.

I have …	Saya punya …
one son	satu anak laki-laki
one daughter	satu anak perempuan
three sons	tiga anak laki-laki
three daughters	tiga anak perempuan

Do you have any brothers and sisters?	Punya kakak atau adik?
How many brothers and sisters do you have?	Berapa saudara anda?
Do you have a boyfriend/ girlfriend?	Punya pacar?

Feelings

I am …	Saya merasa …
angry	marah
bored	bosan
cold	dingin
full	kenyang
happy	senang
hot	panas
hungry	lapar
sad	sedih
scared	takut
sick	sakit
thirsty	haus
tired	lelah/letih

SMALL TALK

Language Problems

Do you speak English?	*Bisa berbicara bahasa Inggris?*
Yes, I do.	*Ya, saya bisa.*
No, I do not.	*Tidak bisa.*
I can only speak a little Indonesian.	*Saya hanya bisa berbicara bahasa Indonesia sedikit.*
Does any one here speak English?	*Ada orang yang bisa bahasa Inggris disini?*
Do you understand?	*Apakah saudara mengerti?*
I understand.	*Saya mengerti.*
I don't understand.	*Saya tidak mengerti.*
How do you say … in Indonesian?	*Apa bahasa Indonesianya …?*
What does this mean?	*Apa artinya ini?*
Please speak slowly!	*Tolong bicara lebih lambat.*
Write that word down for me.	*Tolong tuliskan kata itu untuk saya.*
Please repeat it.	*Tolong ulangi.*
Please translate for me.	*Tolong terjemahkan untuk saya.*

Interests

What is your hobby?	*Apa hobi anda?*
I like …	*Saya suka …*
I do not like …	*Saya tidak suka …*
discos	*disko*
film	*filem*
going shopping	*berbelanja*
music	*musik*
playing games	*bermain game*
playing sport	*berolahraga*
reading books	*membaca buku*

SMALL TALK

to play badminton	*main bulutangkis*
to play soccer	*main sepakbola*
to play table tennis	*main tenis meja*
travelling/going out	*berjalan-jalan*
watching TV	*nonton televisi*

Some Useful Phrases

Look!	*Lihat!*
Listen!	*Dengarlah!*
I am ready.	*Saya siap.*
Slow down!	*Pelan-pelan!*
Hurry up!	*Cepat-cepat!*
Go away!	*Pergi!*
Watch out!	*Awas!*
It is possible.	*Mungkin.*
It is not possible.	*Tidak mungkin.*
I forgot.	*Saya lupa.*
It is important.	*Penting.*
It is not important.	*Tidak penting.*
Where are you going?	*Mau kemana?*
What is this called?	*Apa ini?*
Can I take a photo (of you)?	*Boleh saya potret?*
Can I take a photo (of that)?	*Boleh saya potret itu?*
Do you live here?	*Tinggal di sini?*
It doesn't matter.	*Tidak apa-apa.*

SMALL TALK

Getting Around

Travelling in Indonesia is a slow business, so you don't want to be in a hurry. Departure times are usually approximate, although this is not always so. A lot of projects are underway to improve the condition of the roads but this work is done by manual labour and takes time, so long-distance travel on those bumpy roads can be tedious and uncomfortable. Buses and bemos are usually overcrowded, so if it's at all possible organise yourself to sit in the middle, but not over the wheel, and avoid sitting next to the driver as the gear changes may ruin your kneecaps. If the price is not posted up somewhere, as it usually is for sea travel, you may bargain for a reduction of the fare. If the ticket counter is closed, the head of the bus station or boat office will help you.

Finding Your Way

Where is the ...?	*Dimana ...?*
city bus station	*terminal bis kota*
city bus stop	*halte bis kota*
inter-city bus station	*terminal bis (antar kota)*
train station	*stasiun kereta api*
airport	*lapangan terbang*

What time does the ... leave?	*Jam berapa ... berangkat?*
city bus	*bis kota*
inter-city bus	*bis (antar kota)*
train	*kereta api*
plane	*pesawat udara/pesawat terbang*

37

Directions

How can I get to …?	*Bagaimana saya pergi ke …?*
Is it far?	*Jauh?*
Is it near?	*Dekat?*
Is it near here?	*Dekat dari sini?*
Go straight ahead!	*Jalan terus!*
Turn left …	*Belok kiri …*
Turn right …	*Belok kanan …*
at the T-junction	*di pertigaan*
at the traffic lights	*di lampu lalu lintas*

in front of	*didepan*
next to	*disamping*
behind	*dibelakang*
opposite	*berhadapan dengan*

north	*utara*
south	*selatan*
east	*timur*
west	*barat*
north-west	*(utara) barat laut*
north-east	*(utara) barat laut*
south-west	*barat daya*
south-east	*tenggara*

Air

For internal destinations, surface transportation is much cheaper, and in some cases more easily available, than flights. However you'll find that often the only alternative to a lengthy land or sea passage – particularly in the outer islands – is to take scheduled flights. There can be quite a difference in the fares offered by different agents for the same journey.

How much is a … from Jakarta to Medan?	*Berapa harganya satu … dari Jakarta ke Medan?*
one-way ticket	*tiket satu jalan*
return ticket	*tiket pulang pergi*

| Is there a flight to Medan on Monday? | *Apakah ada pesawat ke Medan pada hari Senin?* |
| What time is the flight to Medan on Monday? | *Jam berapa pesawat berangkat ke Medan pada hari Minggu?* |

GETTING AROUND

I would like to buy a return ticket.	*Saya mau beli satu tiket pulang pergi.*
What time do I have to be at the airport?	*Jam berapa saya harus ada di lapangan udara?*

Bus

The best way to travel long distances is to take an overnight express bus. These buses stop occasionally for meal and toilet stops and can only be boarded at city terminals. Day buses can be hailed or stopped anywhere along the road.

Booking Night Bus Tickets

Where can I buy a night bus ticket?	*Dimana saya bisa beli tiket bis malam?*
Is there any night bus to …?	*Apakah ada bis malam yang ke …?*
What time does the bus arrive at …?	*Jam berapa bisnya sampai/tiba di …?*
Will the bus stop at a restaurant?	*Apakah bisnya akan berhenti di restoran?*
I would like to book a seat for Monday.	*Saya mau pesan satu kursi untuk hari Senin.*

Travelling on a Day Bus

Two tickets to …	*Dua karcis ke …*
Does this bus go to …?	*Apakah bis ini pergi ke …?*
Which bus goes to …?	*Bis yang mana yang ke …?*

What time is the … bus?	*Jam berapa bis yang …?*
next	*berikutnya*
last	*terakhir*

Could you let me know when we arrive at …	*Tolong beritahu saya kalau sudah sampai di …*
I want to get off!	*Saya mau turun! (Kiri!)*

Train

Express and intercity trains usually require booked tickets whereas local train tickets can be bought just before departure.

Please give me two … tickets.	*Minta dua karcis …*
1st class	*kelas satu*
economy class	*kelas ekonomi*

I want to go by express train to …	*Saya mau naik kereta ekspres ke …*
Which platform does the train leave from?	*Dari peron berapa keretanya berangkat?*
Where do I need to change trains?	*Dimana saya harus ganti kereta?*
Is this seat free?	*Kursi ini kosong?*
This seat is taken.	*Sudah ada orangnya*
Would you mind if I open the window?	*Boleh saya buka jendela?*
What is this station called?	*Apa namanya stasiun ini?*
What station is this?	*Ini stasiun apa?*
What is the next station?	*Apa stasiun yang berikutnya?*

Taxi

There are official and unofficial taxis in Indonesia. Official taxis always have a sign and usually a meter, whereas unofficial ones are privately owned cars used illegally as taxis. In taxis without meters, both official and unofficial, you will have to agree on a price before setting out. The official taxis without meters are usually hired hourly or daily.

Please take me to …?	*Tolong antar saya ke …?*
this address	*alamat ini*
the airport	*lapangan terbang*

How much does it cost to go to …?	*Berapa ongkosnya ke …?*
Does that include the luggage?	*Itu termasuk ongkos bagasi?*
That's too much!	*Terlalu mahal!*

Instructions

Here is fine, thank you.	*Berhenti disini.*
The next street, please.	*Jalan berikutnya.*
Continue!	*Terus!*
Please slow down.	*Pelan-pelan saja.*
Please hurry.	*Tolong cepat sedikit.*
Please wait here.	*Tunggu disini.*
I'll be right back.	*Saya akan segera kembali.*

Car

Where can I rent a car?	*Dimana saya bisa sewa mobil?*
How much is it daily/ weekly?	*Berapa ongkos sewanya per hari/minggu?*

Does that include insurance?	*Apa itu termasuk asuransi?*
Where is the next petrol station?	*Dimana pompa bensin yang berikutnya?*
Is this the road to ...?	*Apa ini jalan yang ke ...?*
I want ... litres of petrol.	*Minta ... liter bensin.*
Please fill up the tank.	*Tolong isi penuh.*

Problems

The battery is flat.	*Baterainya habis.*
The radiator is leaking.	*Radiatornya bocor.*
I have a flat tyre.	*Ban saya kempes.*
It is not working.	*Tidak bisa hidup.*
The engine is dead.	*Mesinnya mati.*

Useful Words

battery	*baterai*
brakes	*rem*
car	*mobil*
clutch	*kopeling*
engine	*mesin*
lights	*lampu*
tyres	*ban*
radiator	*radiator*
driver's licence	*SIM (Surat Ijin Mengemudi)*

Signs

No Entry	*dilarang masuk*
No Parking	*dilarang parkir*
One Way	*satu arah*

Local Transport

There's a great variety of local transport in Indonesia. This includes the ubiquitous Balinese *bemo* – a pick-up truck with two rows of seats down the sides or else a small minibus. Bemos usually run standard routes like buses and depart when full, but can also be chartered like a taxi. A step up from the bemo is the small minibus known either as an *oplet, mikrolet* or a *kolt* – since they are often Mitsubishi Colts. In some towns bemos are now known as *angkots*, from *angkutan* (transport) and *kota* (city).

Then there's the *becak*, or bicycle-rickshaw – they're just the same as in so many other Asian countries, but are only found in towns and cities. Increasingly, they are being banned from the central areas of major cities. There are none in Bali. The *bajaj*, a three-wheeler powered by a noisy two-stroke engine, is only found in Jakarta. They're identical to what is known in India as an autorickshaw. In quieter towns, you may find *andongs* and *dokars* – horse or pony carts with two (dokars) or four (andongs) wheels.

Bargaining

How much does it cost to go to …?	*Berapa ongkosnya ke …?*
How about Rp 500?	*Bagaimana kalau Rp 500?*
Here is Rp1000.	*Ini uangnya Rp1000.*
How about my change?	*Mana kembalinya?*

Some Useful Phrases

The (train) is …	*(Kereta)nya …*
delayed (intentional)	*ditunda*
delayed (unexpected)	*tertunda*
cancelled	*dibatalkan*
on time	*tepat*

How long will it be delayed?	*Berapa lama ditundanya/ tertundanya?*
Do I need to change trains?	*Apa saya harus ganti kereta?*
You must change …	*Anda harus ganti …*
How long does the trip take?	*Berapa lama perjalanannya?*
I want to get off at …	*Saya mau turun di …*
I am lost.	*Saya kesasar.*
Where is the nearest bus station?	*Dimana setasiun bis yang terdekat?*
Where can I hire a bicycle?	*Dimana saya bisa sewa sepeda?*
Where do I get off to go to the International Bank?	*Dimana saya harus turun untuk pergi ke Bank Internasional?*
Where are we now?	*Dimana kita sekarang?*
Where is the restroom?	*Dimana kamar kecil?*

GETTING AROUND

Some Useful Words

address	*alamat*
alley	*gang*
airport	*lapangan udara/terbang*
station	*stasiun, terminal bis*
cabin	*ruang*
corner	*sudut/pojok*
confirmation	*penegasan*
dock	*dok*
early	*pagi-pagi*
economy class	*kelas ekonomi*
emergency	*darurat*
empty	*kosong*
fast	*cepat*
full	*penuh*
intersection	*persimpangan*
landing	*pendaratan*
late	*terlambat*
lounge (room)	*kamar tunggu*
plane	*pesawat udara/pesawat terbang*
port	*pelabuhan*
reservation office	*kantor pemesanan*
river	*sungai*
sail	*layar*
sea	*laut*
seat	*tempat duduk*
seat belt/safety belt	*sabuk pengaman*
station master	*kepala stasiun*
steward (f)	*pramugarai*
steward (m)	*pramugara*
street	*jalan*

take off, depart	*berangkat*
timetable	*daftar waktu*
ticket	*karcis/tiket*
ticket window	*loket*
Danger!	*Berbahaya!*
Careful!	*Hati-hati!*
Wait!	*Tunggu!*
Stop!	*Berhenti!/Stop!*

Accommodation

Indonesian hotels range in price and standard from the low to the high end of the market. Hotels of the Hilton and Hyatt style are found in the larger tourist areas. Cheaper and more interesting are the *losmen* – Indonesian hotels – which are also more abundant. The standard of these losmen ranges from very traditional, simple hotels with basic rooms (four walls and a couple of beds) and an outside bathroom *(kamar mandi)*. These days most rooms in losmen have their own bathrooms. Many of these cheap hotels also have a few rooms with showers and air-conditioning available at additional cost. The great advantage of staying in losmen is that you'll meet more Indonesian people.

Finding Accommodation

Where is a ...?	*Dimana ada ...?*
hotel	*hotel*
losmen	*losmen*
cheap hotel	*hotel yang murah*
nice hotel	*hotel yang bagus*
inexpensive hotel	*hotel yang tidak mahal*

I've already found a hotel.	*Saya sudah dapat hotel.*
Please take me to the ... hotel.	*Tolong antar saya ke hotel ...*
What is the address?	*Dimana alamatnya?*
Could you write down the address, please?	*Bisa tolong tulis alamatnya?*

At the Hotel
Checking In

I'd like a room …	*Saya perlu satu kamar …*
for one person	*untuk satu orang*
for two people	*untuk dua orang*
with a bathroom	*dengan kamar mandi*
with a fan	*dengan kipas angin*
with a TV	*dengan TV*
with a window	*dengan jendela*
I am going to stay for …	*Saya mau menginap untuk …*
one day	*satu hari*
one week	*satu minggu*
I'm going to live here for a year.	*Saya mau tinggal disini untuk satu tahun.*
Is there a room available?	*Ada kamar yang kosong?*
How much does it cost per day?	*Berapa biayanya sehari?*
What is the daily rate?	*Berapa tarip hariannya?*
Does the price include breakfast?	*Apa harganya termasuk makan pagi/sarapan?*
Do you allow chidren?	*Boleh saya bawa anak?*
Is there extra cost for children?	*Ada biaya tambahan untuk anak?*
Can I see the room?	*Boleh saya lihat kamarnya?*
I don't like this room.	*Saya tidak suka kamar ini.*
Do you have a better room?	*Ada kamar yang lebih bagus?*
I'll take this room.	*Saya mau kamar ini.*

I'm not sure how long I'm staying.	*Saya tidak tahu berapa lama saya akan menginap disini.*
Should I leave my key in reception?	*Apakah saya perlu tinggalkan kunci kamar di resepsi?*

During Your Stay

Where can I wash my clothes?	*Dimana saya bisa mencuci baju saya?*
Please wash these clothes for me.	*Tolong cuci baju-baju ini.*
When will they be ready?	*Kapan bisa diambil?*
Can I use the telephone?	*Boleh pakai telpon?*
Please spray my room.	*Tolong semprot kamar saya.*
There are mosquitoes in it.	*Ada nyamuk.*
Please change my sheets.	*Tolong ganti spreinya.*
My room needs to be cleaned.	*Tolong bersihkan kamar saya.*

Complaints

Excuse me, I've got a problem here.	*Maaf, ada masalah disini.*
The window is broken.	*Jendelanya rusak.*
I can't open the door/window.	*Saya tidak bisa buka bisapintunya/jendelanya*
I've locked myself out.	*Kunci saya tertinggal di kamar.*
The toilet is broken.	*WCnya rusak.*
Can you get it fixed?	*Bisa diperbaiki?*
The room smells.	*Kamarnya bau.*
It's too dark.	*Terlalu gelap disini.*
It's too noisy.	*Terlalu ribut disini.*

Checking Out

I am leaving this hotel.	*Saya akan meninggalkan hotel ini.*
Please prepare my/our bill.	*Tolong siapkan rekening saya/kami.*
Call me a taxi please.	*Tolong panggilkan taksi.*

Can I pay by …?　　　　　　*Bisa bayar dengan …?*
   credit card　　　　　　　*kartu kredit*
   traveller's cheque　　　　*cek wisata*

Can I leave my things here　*Bisa titit barang-barang saya*
until … ?　　　　　　　　*sampai …?*
   this afternoon　　　　　*nanti siang*
   this evening　　　　　　*nanti sore*
   tonight　　　　　　　　*nanti malam*

Some Useful Phrases

The hotel is near (the) …　　*Hotelnya dekat dari …*
   alley　　　　　　　　　*gang*
   beach　　　　　　　　　*pantai*
   shop　　　　　　　　　*toko*
   street　　　　　　　　　*jalan*
   town square　　　　　　*alun-alun*

I want to have …　　　　　*Saya mau …*
   breakfast　　　　　　　*makan pagi/sarapan*
   lunch　　　　　　　　　*makan siang*
   dinner　　　　　　　　　*makan malam*

I want to drink …   *Saya mau minum …*
   tea   *teh*
   coffee   *kopi*
   boiled water   *air matang*
   cold water   *air dingin*
   fresh water   *air putih*

Some Useful Words

address	*alamat*
air-conditioner	*AC*
	(pronounced: 'ah-say')
bathe (v)	*mandi*
blanket	*selimut*
candle	*lilin*
chair	*kursi*
clean (adj)	*bersih*
crowded	*ramai*
cupboard	*lemari*
dark	*gelap*
dirty	*kotor*
door	*pintu*
dust (n)	*debu*
eat (v)	*makan*
electricity	*listrik*
garden	*kebun*
fence	*pagar*
key, lock	*kunci*
lift	*lift*
mattress	*kasur*
mirror	*kaca/cermin*
noisy	*ribut*

pillow	*bantal*
quiet	*sepi*
rent (v)	*menyewa*
roof	*atap*
servant	*pembantu*
sit (v)	*duduk*
sheet	*seprei*
sleep (v)	*tidur*
soap	*sabun mandi*
soap (detergent)	*sabun cuci*
swimming pool	*kolam renang*
table	*meja*
towel	*handuk*
wake (v)	*bangun*
wash (v)	*cuci*
water	*air*

Around Town

Where is a …	Dimana ada …
bank	*bank*
barber	*tukang cukur*
barong dance	*tari barong*
bookshop	*toko buku*
cinema	*bioskop*
concert	*konser*
consulate	*konsulat*
crossroad	*perempatan*
embassy	*kedutaan besar*
garden	*kebun*
hospital	*rumah sakit*
hotel	*hotel*
market	*pasar*
museum	*musium*
park	*taman*
police station	*kantor polisi*
post office	*kantor pos*
public telephone	*telepon umum*
public toilet	*WC umum*
puppet theatre	*tempat wayang kulit*
restaurant	*rumah makan*
school	*sekolah*
temple	*candi*
theatre	*gedung sandiwara*
town square	*alun-alun*
village	*desa*
zoo	*kebun binatang*

AROUND TOWN

How far is the …?	*Berapa jauh …?*
I am going to the …	*Saya mau pergi ke …*
I want to see the …	*Saya mau lihat …*
I am looking for the …	*Saya mencari …*
What time does it open?	*Jam berapa buka?*
What time does it close?	*Jam berapa tutup?*
Is it still open?	*Masih buka?*

What … is this?	*Ini … apa?*
street	* jalan*
city	* kota*
village	* desa*

At the Post Office

I want to buy …	*Saya mau beli …*
postcards	* kartu pos*
stamps	* perangko*

I want to send a …	*Saya mau kirim …*
letter	* surat*
parcel	* paket*
telegram	* kawat/telegram*

Please send it (by) …	*Tolong kirim dengan/melalui …*
airmail	* pos udara*
surface mail	* pos biasa*
express (overseas)	* ekspres (luar negeri)*
express (domestic)	* kilat (dalam negeri)*

Some Useful Phrases

How much is an airmail letter to the USA?	*Berapa ongkos kirim surat dengan pos udara ke Amerika?*

Please send this parcel to England by surface mail.	*Tolong kirimkan paket ini ke Inggris dengan pos biasa.*
Please weigh this letter.	*Tolong timbang surat ini.*
Please stamp this letter immediately.	*Tolong langsung stempel surat ini*
How much does it cost to send this to …?	*Berapa ongkos kirim ini ke …?*

Some Useful Words

aerogram	*aerogram*
envelope	*amplop*
mailbox	*kotak pos*
postage	*perangko*
receiver (letter)	*penerima*
sender (letter)	*pengirim*

Telephone

I want to call …	*Saya mau menelpon …*
The number is …	*Nomernya …*
I want to speak for three minutes.	*Saya mau bicara untuk tiga menit.*
How much does a three-minute call cost?	*Berapa ongkos telpon untuk tiga menit telpon?*
I want to make a long-distance call to Australia.	*Saya mau menelpon ke Australia.*
I want to make a reverse-charges phone call.	*Saya mau menelpon yang dibayar oleh si penerima.*
Operator, I've been cut off.	*Operator, sambungan telponnya terputus.*
The line is busy.	*Telponnya sedang bicara.*
May I speak to …	*Boleh bicara dengan …*

Sorry, you have the wrong number.	*Maaf, salah nomor.*
Hello, do you speak English?	*Halo, saudara bisa bahasa Inggris?*
Hello, is ... there?	*Halo, ... ada?*
Yes, he/she is here.	*Ya, dia ada.*
One moment, (please).	*(Silakan) tunggu sebentar.*

AROUND TOWN

At the Bank

I want to change ...	*Saya mau menukar ...*
US dollars	*dolar Amerika*
Australian dollars	*dolar Australi*
bank draft	*surat wesel*
cash	*uang kontan*
cheque	*cek*
letter of credit	*surat kredit/LC ('el-ché')*
money	*uang*
travellers' cheque	*cek turis*

Some Useful Phrases

What time do banks open?	*Jam berapa bank buka?*
What time does the bank open?	*Jam berapa banknya buka?*
Where can I cash a travellers' cheque?	*Dimana saya bisa menguangkan cek perjalanan turis?*
What is the exchange rate?	*Berapa kursnya?*
Has any money arrived for me?	*Ada kiriman uang untuk saya?*
Can I transfer money here from my bank?	*Bisakah menransfer uang dari bank saya ke sini?*
How long will it take to arrive?	*Berapa lama untuk sampai kesitu?*

Some Useful Words

bank clerk	*pegawai bank*
bill, note	*uang kertas*
branch	*cabang*
coins	*uang logam*
commission	*komisi*
endorsement	*pengesyahan*
ID card	*K.T.P.*
signature	*tanda tangan*
teller	*kasir*
ticket window	*loket*

Sightseeing

Where is the tourist office?	*Dimana ada kantor wisata?*
What is that building?	*Itu gedung apa?*
What is this monument?	*Ini monumen apa?*
Who lived there?	*Dulu siapa yang tinggal di sana?*
Do you have a local map?	*Saudara punya peta lokal?*
May I take photographs?	*Boleh saya ambil foto?*
May I take your photograph?	*Boleh saya foto saudara?*
I will send you the photograph.	*Saya akan kirim fotonya kepada saudara.*
Could you take a photograph of me?	*Bisa tolong foto saya?*
At what theatre can I see a play?	*Di teater mana saya bisa menonton sandiwara?*
How did you enjoy the play?	*Apakah saudara suka sandiwara itu?*
I'm interested in music.	*Saya suka musik.*

Some Useful Words

castle	*benteng*
church	*gereja*
crowded (noisy)	*ramai*
empty	*kosong*
interesting	*menarik hati*
mosque	*mesjid*
nice	*bagus*
quiet	*sepi*
statue	*patung*
ticket	*karcis*
university	*universitas*
nightclub	*kelab malam*

AROUND TOWN

Bureaucracy

If you need to have dealings with the Indonesian bureaucracy for
any reason, there are a couple of things you ought to remember.
Always dress decently. Try to speak to the person in charge – you
will get more information this way and there is a good chance they
will speak some English. With their English and your Indonesian
you shouldn't have too many problems. In descending order of
importance the official titles are:

head of province	*bupati*
head of a district	*camat*
head of an area	*kepala desa*
village chief	*kepala kampung*

Forms

name	*nama*
address	*alamat*

date of birth	*tanggal lahir*
place of birth	*tempat lahir*
age	*umur*
sex	*jenis kelamin*
nationality	*kebangsaan*
religion	*agama*
profession	*pekerjaan*
reason for travel	*maksud kunjungan*
marital status	*status perkawinan*
single	*belum kawin*
married	*kawin*
divorced	*cerai*
widow	*janda*
widower	*duda*
identification	*surat keterangan*
passport number	*nomor paspor*
visa	*visa*
birth certificate	*surat keterangan lahir*
driver's licence	*S.I.M. (Surat Ijin Mengemudi)*
customs	*bea cukai*
immigration	*imigrasi*
purpose of visit	*maksud kunjungan*
holiday	*liburan*
business	*pekerjaan*
visiting relatives	*kunjungan keluarga*

In the Country

When you go camping or hiking in Indonesia, you will discover that most directions are given in terms of compass points – left and right are not used very often in the country. The compass points are:

north	*utara*
south	*selatan*
east	*timur*
west	*barat*
north-west	*barat laut*
north-east	*timur laut*
south-west	*barat daya*
south-east	*tenggara*

Indonesians are very polite people and like to be agreeable. If you simply ask 'Is this north?', they may just agree with you, so it's preferable to use *Dimana utara?*, Where is north?, to get your bearings. If there is any doubt, ask several different people. Remember that in Bali 'north' traditionally means 'towards the mountains'.

Weather

What's the weather like?	*Bagaimana cuacanya?*
Today it is …	*Hari ini …*
cloudy	*mendung*
cold	*dingin*

61

flooding	*banjir*
hot	*panas*
humid	*lembab*
raining heavily	*hujan lebat*
raining lightly	*gerimis*
warm	*hangat*
wet	*basah*
windy	*berangin*

What time is …?	*Jam berapa …?*
sunrise	*matahari terbit*
sunset	*matahari terbenam*

Some Useful Words

cloud	*awan*
dry season	*musim kemarau*
earth	*bumi*
fog	*kabut*
moon	*bulan*
mud	*lumpur*
rain	*hujan*
rainy season	*musim hujan*
sky	*langit*
smoke	*asap*
storm	*badai*
sun	*matahari*
	(literally: eye of the day)

Geographical Terms

beach	*pantai*
bridge	*jembatan*

cave	*gua/goa*
city	*kota*
estuary	*kuala*
forest	*hutan*
harbour	*pelabuhan*
hill	*bukit*
hot spring	*mata air panas*
island	*pulau*
lake	*danau*
mountain	*gunung*
plain	*dataran*
river	*sungai*
sea	*laut*
valley	*lembah*
village	*desa*
waterfall	*air terjun*

IN THE COUNTRY

Plants & Agriculture

agriculture	*pertanian*
cloves	*cengkeh*

IN THE COUNTRY

coconut palm	*pohon kelapa*
corn	*jagung*
firewood	*kayu bakar*
flower	*bunga*
fruit tree	*pohon buah*
harvest (v)	*panen*
irrigation	*pengairan*
leaf	*daun*
planting	*menanam*
rice field	*sawah*
rice terrace	*petak sawah*
sugar cane	*tebu*
tobacco	*tembakau*

Animals & Birds

bird	*burung*
buffalo	*kerbau*
cat	*kucing*
chicken	*ayam*
cow	*sapi*
crocodile	*buaya*
dog	*anjing*
fish	*ikan*
frog	*katak*
goat	*kambing*
horse	*kuda*
leech	*lintah*
lion	*singa*
monkey	*monyet*
pig	*babi*
rooster	*ayam jantan*

sheep	*domba*
snake	*ular*
spider	*laba-laba*
tiger	*harimau*

Insects

ant	*semut*
butterfly	*kupu-kupu*
cockroach	*kecoa*
fly	*lalat*
mosquito	*nyamuk*

IN THE COUNTRY

Outdoor Activities

mountain climbing	*mendaki gunung*
diving	*menyelam*
fishing	*memancing*
hunting	*berburuh*
surfing	*bermain selancar*
swimming	*berenang*

Some Useful Words

backpack	*ransel*
campground	*tempat kemah*
camping	*berkemah*
compass	*kompas*
mat	*tikar*
penknife	*pisau lipat*
rope	*tali/tambang*
stove	*kompor*
tent	*tenda*
torch (flashlight)	*senter*

IN THE COUNTRY

Some Useful Phrases

Are there any tourist attractions near here?	*Ada tempat pariwisata dekat sini?*
Is it safe to swim here?	*Aman berenang disini?*
There are two caves here.	*Ada dua gua/goa disini.*
Where is the nearest village?	*Dimana desa yang paling dekat?*
Is it safe to climb this mountain?	*Aman mendaki gunung ini?*
Is there a hut up there?	*Apakah ada pondok di atas?*
Do I need a guide?	*Apakah saya perlu pemandu wisata?*

Food

The simplicity of the Indonesian language is very easy to see when it comes to words connected with food and eating. *Makan* is both the verb 'to eat' and a general word concerning food. A restaurant is an 'eating house', *rumah makan*. Breakfast is 'morning food', *makan pagi*. In addition you will find that eating out in Indonesia is a very informal affair. There are basically three options: hotel restaurants where the food is expensive but not necessarily the best; *warung*, the temporary food stalls which are set up every morning or evening and usually serve the best genuine local delicacies at low prices; and the intermediate option, which is to visit one of the host of local restaurants which line the main street of any town.

FOOD

Where is a …	*Dimana ada …*
cheap restaurant	*rumah makan murah*
restaurant	*rumah makan*
food stall	*warung*
night market	*pasar malam*

At the Restaurant

We would like a table for five, please.	*Minta meja untuk lima orang.*
Is there a table for five available?	*Ada meja untuk lima orang.*
Please bring …	*Boleh minta …*
the menu	*daftar makanan*
a glass of water	*segelas air putih*
the bill	*bon*

68

I can't eat …	*Saya tidak boleh makan …*
milk and cheese	*susu dan keju*
eggs	*telur*
meat	*daging*
prawns	*udang*

This isn't cooked properly.	*Ini belum matang.*
Not too spicy please.	*Jangan terlalu pedas, ya.*
No MSG please.	*Jangan pakai Aji-ni-moto/*
	bumbu masak.
This is delicious.	*Makanan ini enak.*

At the Market

The market is the dynamic focal point of life in any Indonesian town. In the market the most intriguing array of local produce will be laid out for sale, including all the locally grown fruits. Although the greatest range of fruits is available in the wet season, there is always some fresh fruit on offer.

There are always bananas, *pisang*, which are found in a multitude of forms, and are about the cheapest fruit. Rambutans, *rambutan*, are a bright red fruit covered in soft, hairy spines, and containing a delicious, lychee-like, sweet white flesh. The mangosteen, *manggis*, is very sought after for its mouth-watering sweet-sour white flesh, and is easily recognised by its thick purple-brown fibrous outer covering which protects the segmented fruit inside.

Don't let the perfect brown 'snakeskin' covering deter you from buying and trying a few *salak*. They are the fruit of the Zalacca palm and the flesh is crunchy and nutty in flavour. Jackfruit *(nangka)* trees are widely grown in homegardens, and can be recognised by huge pendulous fruit, often wrapped in a large plastic bag for protection while they ripen on the tree. Jackfruit sellers often break the whole fruit up into individual segments, which are then packed, ready to eat, into small plastic bags for sale in the market. The flesh is rubbery and sweet, and rather strongly flavoured.

An encounter with a durian, *durian*, the 'king of fruits', is a most memorable experience for the fruit lover. Durians announce themselves in any market by exuding an incredibly pungent stench. If you can hold your breath long enough to approach, and swallow the rich, creamy flesh, you will get to appreciate an absolutely unique flavour.

Starfruit, *belimbing*, is a watery thirst-quenching fruit, shaped like a star when viewed end on. It is one of the few fruits which are eaten without being peeled or having their outer covering removed. A good wash in boiled water is advisable.

FOOD

Most tropical fruits are soft, even mushy, so it's a refreshing change to find a crunchy, almost woody textured fruit, such as the guava or *jambu*. It is a hard, pear-shaped fruit, with small black seeds which should not be eaten.

There are other more familiar fruits available as well. Mangoes, *mangga*, when in season are delicious; pineapples, *nanas*, are invariably extremely sweet, and lacking the acid bite we often associate with pineapples grown in temperate climates; while coconuts, *kelapa*, are very familiar to most Indonesians. The young coconut, *kelapa muda*, lopped off the nearest coconut palm makes a delightfully refreshing, naturally sterile drink. Pawpaws, *papaya*, are ubiquitous and can be found in a number of different varieties.

An unusual fruit salad made from the unripe flesh of the pawpaw, mango, jambu, pineapple or starfruit is a favourite of the Javanese. It is sweetened with palm sugar and flavoured with ground chillies. Green fruit and fresh chillies present a challenge to a weak stomach – take care!

How much is a kg of …?	*Berapa sekilo …?*
A kg of …, please.	*Minta sekilo …*
I don't want that one.	*Jangan yang itu.*
Please give me another one.	*Tolong kasih saya yang lainnya.*

Meals
breakfast	*makan pagi/sarapan*
lunch	*makan siang*
dinner	*makan malam*

Meat — *Daging*
beef	*daging sapi*
brains	*otak*
chicken	*ayam*
duck	*daging bebek*
heart	*jantung*
lamb	*domba*
liver	*hati*
mutton, goat	*kambing*

Fruit & Nuts — *Buah & Kacang*
apples	*apel*
banana	*pisang*
cempedak	*cempedak – similar to a jackfruit but sweeter, more tender*
coconut	*kelapa*
durian	*durian*
jackfruit	*nangka*
lemon	*jeruk nipis*
mangosteen	*manggis*
mango	*mangga*
orange	*jeruk manis*
pawpaw	*papaya*
peanuts	*kacang*
pineapple	*nanas*
starfruit	*belimbing*
strawberry	*arbei*

FOOD

Vegetables   Sayur

Most vegetables are simply called *sayur*, without having an individual name. If you are a vegetarian you can say *tanpa daging*, without meat, or *sayur saja*, vegetables only.

beans	*buncis*
cabbage	*kol*
carrot	*wortel*
cauliflower	*bunga kol*
corn	*jagung*
cucumber	*ketimun*
eggplant	*terong*
mushrooms	*jamur*
onion	*bawang bombay*
potato	*kentang*
pumpkin	*labu merah*
tomato	*tomat*

Staples

bread	*roti tawar*
noodles	*mie*
rice (cooked)	*nasi*

Snacks

biscuits	*biskit*
egg	*telur*
boiled egg	*telur rebus*
fried egg	*telur goreng*
poached egg	*telur ceplok*
omelette	*telur dadar*
cake	*kue*
sweets	*manisan*

FOOD

Spices & Condiments

chilli	*cabe*
cinnamon	*kayu manis*
cloves	*cengkeh*
curry	*kari*
garlic	*bawang putih*
ginger	*jahe*
oil	*minyak*
pepper	*lada*
salt	*garam*
soy sauce	*kecap asin*
sweet soy sauce	*kecap manis*
sugar	*gula*
turmeric	*kunyit*
vinegar	*cuka*

Seafood — *Ikan*

crab	*kepiting*
freshwater fish	*ikan tambak*
lobster	*udang karang*
mussels	*kerang*
oysters	*tiram*
saltwater fish	*ikan laut*
shrimp	*udang*
squid	*cumi-cumi*

Drinks
Cold Drinks

beer	*bir*
boiled water	*air matang*
plain water	*air putih*

FOOD

chocolate	*coklat*
citrus juice	*es jeruk*
coconut milk	*es kelapa*
cordial	*sirup*
ginger tea	*teh jahe*
milk	*susu*
rice wine	*brem*

Hot Drinks

coffee	*kopi*
tea	*teh*
with/without milk	*dengan/tanpa susu*
with/without sugar	*dengan/tanpa gula*

Cooking Methods

baked	*panggang*
boiled	*rebus*
fried	*goreng*
grilled	*bakar*
steamed	*kukus*
smoked	*asap*

Special Dishes

Every region of Indonesia has its own special dishes, which you will want to try out. The best place to find the local dishes is at the food stalls along the street, because that's where the local people eat. Just go along and see what is being served.

chicken soup	*sop ayam*
cooked vegetables with peanut sauce	*gado-gado*
meat grilled on skewers	*sate*
mixed vegetables (Chinese dish)	*cap cai*
noodle soup	*mie kuah*
pancake with accompaniments	*martabak*
raw vegetables, salted	*asinan*
rice (uncooked)	*beras*
rice (cooked)	*nasi*
boiled or steamed rice	*nasi putih*
fried rice	*nasi goreng*
rice and vegetables	*nasi sayur*
rice with a selection of things, including meat	*nasi campur*
roast lamb	*kambing guling*
roast piglet	*babi guling*

Some Useful Words

ashtray	*asbak*
bitter	*pahit*
boil (v)	*merebus*
boiled	*rebus*

FOOD

cold	*dingin*
cook (v)	*masak*
delicious	*enak*
eat (v)	*makan*
foreign	*asing*
fresh	*segar*
fry (v)	*goreng*
good (food)	*enak*
hot	*panas*
indigenous	*asli*
salty	*asin*
slice (v)	*iris*
sour	*asam*
spicy	*pedas*
sweet	*manis*
toothpick	*tusuk gigi*
unripe/uncooked	*mentah*

FOOD

Some Useful Phrases

I'm sorry but this table is reserved.	*Maaf, tapi meja ini sudah dipesan.*
We're in a hurry. Please bring our food quickly.	*Kami terburu-buru. Tolong bawa makanan kami, secepatnya.*
May we have our bill please?	*Tolong kasih bonnya.*

Shopping

In Indonesia it is customary to bargain, but this is mainly in the market or for services like taxis and pedicabs. In shops and restaurants, or wherever prices are marked on the items, bargaining is not customary. This is known as fixed price or *harga pas*. It is quite common for tourists to be charged more than the local people, as they are often considered to be wealthy. Even so, tourists do not usually pay a great deal more than the locals and if you want to know the common price, *harga biasa*, ask an independent bystander. On the public transport system watch what everybody else is paying. For long trips, or boat trips, expect to pay a little more than the locals. Bargaining is part of the way of life in Indonesia. If you treat it like a game it can be fun, even worthwhile, but remember that the 500 rupiah price difference you may be getting so upset about is really only a few cents to you.

Useful Shops & Items

Where is the …?	*Dimana ada …?*
barber	*tukang cukur rambut*
bookshop	*toko buku*
chemist	*apotik*
grocery	*toko makanan*
market	*pasar*
night market	*pasar malam*
shopping centre	*pusat pertokoan*
tailor	*penjahit*

I want to buy …	*Saya mau beli …*
that basket	*keranjang itu*
this bottle	*botol ini*

buttons	*kancing*
combs	*sisir*
jar	*toples*
mosquito net	*kelambu*
needle	*jarum*
rope	*tambang/tali*
sarong	*kain sarung*
scissors	*gunting*
shoelaces	*tali sepatu*
suitcase	*kopor*
swimsuit	*baju renang*
thread	*benang*
torch (flashlight)	*senter*
towel	*handuk*

SHOPPING

Bargaining

Can I bargain?	*Boleh tawar?*
That's very expensive.	*Mahal sekali.*
I don't have much money.	*Saya tidak ada banyak uang.*
Can you lower the price?	*Boleh kurang?*
I'll give you …	*Saya bayar …*
No more than …	*Tidak lebih dari …*

Souvenirs

bone	*tulang*
bracelet	*gelang*
earrings	*anting-anting*
gold	*emas*
handicraft	*kerajinan tangan*
handmade batik	*batik tulis*
horn	*tanduk*
ivory	*gading*
jewellery	*perhiasan*
leather	*kulit*
masks	*topeng*
material	*kain*
necklace	*kalung*
paintings	*lukisan*
pottery	*keramik*
printed batik	*batik cap*
puppets	*wayang kulit*
ring	*cincin*
silver	*perak*
souvenir	*kenang-kenangan*
statue	*patung*
stone carvings	*ukiran batu*
woodcarving	*ukiran kayu*

SHOPPING

Clothing

bras	**be**ha
cardigan	mantel
clothing	pakaian
dress	baju
gloves	sarung tangan
hat	topi
jacket	jaket
jeans	jean
jumper	ka0s hangat
sandals	sandal
shirt	kemeja
shorts	celana pendek
shoes	sepatu
skirt	rok
socks	kaos kaki
thongs/flip flops	sandal jepit
tie	dasi
trousers	celana panjang
T-shirt	kaos
underpants	celana dalam
underwear	pakaian dalam

SHOPPING

Materials

cotton	*katun*
leather	*kulit*
silk	*sutra*
wool	*wol*

Stationery & Publications

ballpoint pen	*bolpoin*
a bilingual dictionary	*kamus dua bahasa*
envelopes	*amplop*
a magazine	*majalah*
map	*peta*
the morning newspaper	*koran pagi*
English newspaper	*koran bahasa Inggris*
novel	*novel*
a pocket dictionary	*kamus saku*
scissors	*gunting*
writing paper	*kertas tulis*

Toiletries

baby's bottle	*botol bayi*
baby powder	*bedak bayi*
condoms	*kondom*
contraceptive	*kontrasepsi*
laxative	*obat cuci perut*
moisturising cream	*krim pelembab*
mosquito repellent	*obat nyamuk*
razor blade	*silet*
sanitary napkins	*duk/softex*
shampoo	*sampo*
shaver	*pisau cukur*

SHOPPING

shaving cream	*krim cukur*
sunblock cream	*krim pengangkal terbakar sinar matahari*
tampons	*tampon*
tissues	*tisu*
toilet paper	*kertas kamar kecil*
toothbrush	*sikat gigi*
toothpaste	*odol/pasta gigi*

Photography

I'd like a film for this camera.	*Minta filem untuk kamera ini.*
How much is it for processing and developing?	*Berapa ongkos cuci cetak?*
When will it be ready?	*Kapan selesainya?*
Do you repair cameras here?	*Bisa memperbaiki kamera disini?*

B&W (film)	*(filem) hitam/putih*
camera	*kamera*
colour (film)	*(filem) berwarna*
to develop	*mencuci*
film	*filem*
photograph	*foto*

Smoking

cigarettes	*rokok*
matches	*korek api*
pipe	*pipa rokok*
tobacco	*tembakau*
A packet of cigarettes, please.	*Minta rokok satu bungkus.*
Do you have a light?	*Boleh minta api?*

SHOPPING

Weights & Measures

gm	*gram*
kg	*kg*
mm	*milimeter*
cm	*sentimeter*
meter	*meter*
km	*kilometer*
litre	*liter*

Sizes & Comparisons

big	*besar*
bigger	*lebih besar*
biggest	*paling besar*
too big	*terlalu besar/kebesaran*
very big	*sangat besar*
small	*kecil*
smaller	*lebih kecil*
smallest	*paling kecil*
too small	*terlalu kecil/kekecilan*
very small	*sangat kecil*
enough	*cukup*
less	*kurang*
more	*lebih (banyak)*
heavy	*berat*
light	*ringan*
long	*panjang*
short	*pendek*
tall	*tinggi*
wide	*lebar*
narrow	*sempit*

Colours

black	*hitam*
blue	*biru*
brown	*coklat*
colour	*warna*
dark	*tua*
green	*hijau*
light	*muda*
orange	*jingga*
pink	*merah muda*
purple	*ungu*
red	*merah*
white	*putih*
yellow	*kuning*

Some Useful Words

big	*besar*
buy (v)	*beli*
cheap	*murah*
discount	*korting*
expensive	*mahal*
export (v)	*mengekspor*
import (v)	*mengimpor*
like (v)	*suka*
made in (country)	*buatan*
old	*tua*
order (v)	*pesan*
parcel	*bungkusan*
prefer	*lebih suka*
quality	*kwalitas*
quantity	*jumlah*

SHOPPING

round	*bulat*
sell	*jual*
small	*kecil*
style	*macam*
want (v)	*mau*

Some Useful Phrases

I'm just looking.	*Saya hanya lihat-lihat.*
What is the normal price of this?	*Berapa harga biasanya?*
Can you write down the price?	*Bisa tolong tulis harganya.*
Do you accept credit cards?	*Bisa bayar dengan kartu kredit?*
May I try this on?	*Boleh saya coba?*
Do you have others?	*Ada yang lain?*
We don't have any.	*Tidak ada lagi.*
Can I see it?	*Boleh saya lihat?*
I don't like it.	*Saya tidak suka ini.*
I will take it.	*Saya beli yang ini.*
I'd like to look at blouses.	*Saya ingin melihat-lihat blus.*
How much is this?	*Berapa harganya ini?*
Where are these goods made?	*Barang-barang ini buatan mana?*
Do I need insurance?	*Apakah saya perlu asuransi?*
free of charge	*gratis*

SHOPPING

Health

With luck your time in Indonesia will be without illness and you will not need to turn to this section at all.

Sakit is an all-purpose word about illness. As a verb *sakit* means 'to feel sick' or 'to hurt', as an adjective it means 'sick' or 'painful'. For example: the hospital, *rumah sakit;* I am ill, *Saya sakit.*

Where is a ...	*Dimana ada ...*
dentist	*doktergigi*
doctor	*dokter*
hospital	*rumah sakit*
medicine	*obat*
pharmacy	*apotik*

At the Doctor

I'm suffering from ...	*Saya sakit ...*
I am allergic to ...	*Saya alergi ...*
My ... hurts	*... saya sakit.*
I feel nauseous.	*Saya mau muntah.*
I keep vomiting.	*Saya muntah terus.*
I feel dizzy.	*Saya merasa pusing.*

I'm allergic to penicillin/ antibiotics.	*Saya alergi penisilin/antibiotika.*
I have low/high blood pressure.	*Saya menderita tekanan darah rendah/tinggi.*
Could I see a female doctor?	*Ada dokter perempuan disini?*

87

Could I see a doctor for females?	*Ada dokter untuk perempuan disini?*
I'm pregnant.	*Saya hamil.*
I'm on the pill.	*Saya pakai pil kontrasepsi.*
I haven't menstruated for … weeks.	*Saya belum mentruasi selama … minggu.*
I've been vaccinated.	*Saya sudah divaksinasi.*
I have my own syringe.	*Saya punya suntikan saya sendiri.*
I've had a blood test.	*Saya sudah periksa darah.*
I need a blood test.	*Saya perlu periksa darah.*
Please use this syringe.	*Pakai suntikan ini.*
How many times a day?	*Berapa kali sehari?*

Ailments

allergy	*alergi*
asthma	*asma*
burns	*luka bakar*
cholera	*kolera*
cold	*masuk angin*
constipation	*sukar buang air besar*
cough (v)	*batuk*
diarrhoea	*diare/mencret*
dysentery	*disentri*
fever	*demam*
flu	*selesma*
food poisoning	*keracunan makanan*
headache	*sakit kepala*
hepatitis	*hepatitis*
high blood pressure	*darah tinggi*
infection	*infeksi*

HEALTH

itch	*gatal*
lice	*kutu*
malaria	*malaria*
pain	*sakit*
rabies	*rabies*
rheumatism	*encok*
sore throat	*sakit tenggorokan*
stomachache	*sakit perut*
sunburn	*kulit terbakar matahari*
typhoid	*demam tipus*
venereal disease	*penyakit kelamin*
worms	*cacingan*
wound	*luka*

Parts of the Body

arm	*lengan*
back	*punggung*
bone	*tulang*
breast	*buah dada*
chest	*dada*
chin	*dagu*
ear	*telinga*
eye	*mata*
face	*wajah/muka*
finger	*jari tangan*
hands	*tangan*
head	*kepala*
heart	*jantung*
hip	*pinggul*
kidney	*ginjal*
leg/foot	*kaki*

HEALTH

liver	*hati*
lung	*paru-paru*
mouth	*mulut*
muscle	*otot*
neck	*leher*
nose	*hidung*
shoulder	*bahu/pundak*
skin	*kulit*
stomach	*perut*
toes	*jari kaki*
tooth	*gigi*

Medicine

antibiotics	*antibiotisk*
antiseptic	*antiseptik*
aspirin	*aspirin*
penicillin	*penisilin*
quinine	*kina*
sleeping pills	*pil tidur*
tablet	*tablet*
vitamins	*vitamin*

Some Useful Words

accident	*kecelakaan*
addiction	*kecanduan*
allergic	*alergi*
bandage	*pembalut/perban*
bleed (v)	*berdarah*
blood	*darah*
broken	*patah*
breath	*nafas*

burn (v)	*bakar*
careful	*hati-hati*
collapse/faint (v)	*jatuh/pingsan*
compress	*kompres*
contraceptive	*kontrasepsi*
dog bite	*gigitan anjing*
disease	*penyakit*
faeces	*buang air besar*
fast (v, n)	*puasa*
health	*kesehatan*
injection	*suntikan*
menstruation	*menstruasi*
oxygen	*oksigen*
poisonous	*beracun*
prescription	*resep*
urine	*air seni*
vomit (v)	*muntah*

At the Chemist

I need medicine for …	*Saya perlu obat untuk …*
(Do) I need a prescription for …	*(Apakah) Saya perlu resep untuk …*
These tablets must be taken three times a day.	*Tablet-tablet ini harus diminum tiga kali sehari.*
Please shake the bottle before taking.	*Kocok dulu sebelum diminum.*

At the Dentist

My tooth hurts.	*Gigi saya sakit.*
I've lost a filling.	*Tambalan gigi saya rusak.*
I've broken a tooth.	*Gigi saya patah.*
My gums hurt.	*Gusi saya sakit.*
I don't want it extracted.	*Jangan dicabut.*
Please give me an anaesthetic.	*Tolong beri saya obat matirasa.*

Some Useful Phrases

Please take us to a hospital.	*Tolong antar kami ke rumah sakit.*
Please buy medicine for me at the pharmacy.	*Tolong beli obat untuk saya di apotik.*
My leg is broken.	*Kaki saya patah.*
I need a receipt for my insurance.	*Saya perlu kwitansi untuk asuransi saya.*

HEALTH

Time & Dates

Telling the Time

Telling the time in Indonesia is fairly straightforward. The English 'am' and 'pm' are replaced by whole words rather than abbreviations. For example, '8 am' is literally *jam delapan pagi*, '8 in the morning'; '8 pm' is *jam delapan malam*, '8 at night'.

hour	*jam*
minute	*menit*
second	*detik*
plus (past)	*lewat*
minus (to)	*kurang*
half	*setengah*

What time is it?	*Jam berapa (sekarang)?*
It is three o'clock.	*Jam tiga.*
It is a quarter to four.	*Jam empat kurang seperempat.*
It is a quarter past four.	*Jam empat lewat seperempat*
It is ten past three.	*Jam tiga lewat sepuluh.*
It is ten to four.	*Jam empat kurang sepuluh.*

Unlike English, five thirty is not given in Indonesian as half past five but as half to six.

It is five-thirty.	*Jam setengah enam.*

one/an hour	*satu jam*
two hours	*dua jam*
three hours	*tiga jam*

TIMES, DATES & FESTIVALS

o'clock	*jam*
in the morning (1 – 11 am)	*pagi*
in the afternoon (11 am – 3 pm)	*siang*
in the evening (3 – 6 pm)	*sore*
at night (6 – 12 pm)	*malam*

Days of the Week

Monday	*hari Senin*
Tuesday	*hari Selasa*
Wednesday	*hari Rabu*
Thursday	*hari Kamis*
Friday	*hari Jum'at*
Saturday	*hari Sabtu*
Sunday	*hari Minggu*

On Monday.	*Pada hari Senin.*

Months

January	*Januari*
February	*Februari*
March	*Maret*
April	*April*
May	*Mei*
June	*Juni*
July	*Juli*
August	*Agustus*
September	*September*
October	*Oktober*
November	*Nopember*
December	*Desember*

During June.	*Selama bulan Juni.*

Dates

The number of the day precedes the name of the month in Indonesian dates.

17 August 1945 (Independence Day)	*tujuhbelas Agustus sembilanbelas empatpuluh lima (Hari Kemerdekaan)*

Some Useful Phrases

What date is it today?	*Tanggal berapa hari ini?*
It's 28 June.	*Tanggal duapuluh delapan Juni.*
It's 1 April.	*Tanggal satu April.*
When did you arrive in Indonesia?	*Kapan tiba di Indonesia?*
Two weeks ago.	*Dua minggu yang lalu.*
How long will you stay?	*Berapa lama anda akan tinggal?*
I'll be staying (another) two weeks.	*Saya akan tinggal dua minggu lagi.*

Present

today	*hari ini*
this morning	*pagi ini*
this afternoon	*siang ini*
tonight	*malam ini*
this week	*minggu ini*
this month	*bulan ini*
this year	*tahun ini*
now	*sekarang*
immediately	*sekarang juga*
just now	*baru saja*

Past

yesterday	*kemarin*
day before yesterday	*kemarin dulu*
yesterday morning	*kemarin pagi*
yesterday afternoon	*kemarin siang*
last night	*tadi malam/kemarin malam*
last week	*minggu lalu*
last month	*bulan lalu*
last year	*tahun lalu*
ago	*yang lalu*
already	*sudah*

Future

tomorrow	*besok*
tomorrow morning	*besok pagi*
tomorrow evening	*besok sore*
day after tomorrow	*lusa*
next week	*minggu depan*
next month	*bulan depan*
next year	*tahun depan*
later	*nanti*
after	*sesudah*
not yet	*belum*

During the Day

sunrise	*matahari terbit*
dawn	*pagi buta*
noon	*tengah hari*
sunset	*matahari terbenam*
midnight	*tengah malam*

Some Useful Words

as soon as possible	*secepatnya*
a while ago	*beberapa waktu yang lalu*
a moment	*sebentar*
after	*sesudah*
always	*selalu*
before	*sebelum*
century	*abad*
day	*hari*
early	*awal*
everyday	*setiap hari*
forever	*selamanya*

fortnight	*dua minggu*
long ago	*dulu*
month	*bulan*
never	*tidak pernah*
not any more	*tidak lagi*
not yet	*belum*
recently	*baru-baru ini*
sometimes	*kadang-kadang*
soon	*segera*
week	*minggu*
year	*tahun*

Numbers & Amounts

Indonesian numbers are quite straightforward. Numbers from 11 to 19 are comprised of the numbers one to nine plus the suffix *belas*. Numbers after that are counted with the suffix of 10 – *puluh*. *Sepuluh* is 10, *duapuluh* is 20 and so on until the hundreds, when the suffix *ratus* is used. So *seratus* is 100, *duaratus* is 200, and so on. *Ribu* is the suffix for thousands, and *juta* is the suffix for millions.

99

Cardinal Numbers

0	*nol*	19	*sembilanbelas*
1	*satu*	20	*duapuluh*
2	*dua*	21	*duapuluh satu*
3	*tiga*	22	*duapuluh dua*
4	*empat*	30	*tigapuluh*
5	*lima*	40	*empatpuluh*
6	*enam*	50	*limapuluh*
7	*tujuh*	100	*seratus*
8	*delapan*	200	*duaratus*
9	*sembilan*	300	*tigaratus*
10	*sepuluh*	1000	*seribu*
11	*sebelas*	2000	*duaribu*
12	*duabelas*	3000	*tigaribu*
13	*tigabelas*	1 million	*sejuta*
14	*empatbelas*	2 million	*dua juta*
15	*limabelas*		
16	*enambelas*		
17	*tujuhbelas*		
18	*delapanbelas*		

268	*duaratus enampuluh delapan*
51,783	*limapuluhsaturibu, tujuhratus delapanpuluh tiga*

Fractions

½	*setengah*
⅓	*sepertiga*
¼	*seperempat*
¾	*tiga per empat*

NUMBERS

Ordinal Numbers

1st	*pertama*
2nd	*kedua*
3rd	*ketiga*
4th	*keempat*
5th	*kelima*
6th	*keenam*
7th	*ketujuh*
8th	*kedelapan*
9th	*kesembilan*
10th	*kesepuluh*

the first bus	*bis (yang) pertama*
the third building	*gedung (yang) ketiga*

Quantity

about	*kira-kira*
a little (amount)	*sedikit*
to count	*menghitung*
double	*dobel*
a dozen	*selusin*
enough	*cukup*
few	*sedikit*
many	*banyak*
minus	*kurang*
more	*lebih*
number	*nomor*
one more	*satu lagi*
plus	*tambah*
a pair	*sepasang*

NUMBERS

percent	*persen*
quantity	*jumlah*
too expensive	*terlalu mahal/kemahalan*
very expensive	*sangat mahal*

NUMBERS

Bahasa Indonesia & Bahasa Malaysia

Although the national languages of Indonesia and Malaysia are both based on the same language, known as Malay, the languages have diverged and are developing in somewhat different directions. Many traditional Malay words are falling out of use in Indonesia and are being replaced or supplemented by new words borrowed from Javanese and English, amongst other sources.

You will find, however, that your knowledge of Bahasa Indonesia will form a good basis for travelling in Malaysia and learning Malaysia's language.

The structures and grammars remain common to both languages – the differences are in vocabulary. Unfortunately the different vocabularies include many commonly used words which crop up in many sentences. In most cases your Bahasa Indonesia will be well understood and will probably just be considered a source of amusement. The following are some of the most prominent differences between modern Bahasa Malaysia and Bahasa Indonesia. Many of these differences are not reflected in dictionaries of the languages, but are different in common usage.

English	Indonesian	Malaysian
aeroplane	*pesawat udara*	*kapalterbang*
after	*sesudah*	*selepas*
afternoon	*sore*	*petang*
always	*selalu*	*senantiasa*
beef	*daging sapi*	*daging lembu*
brother	*kakak/adik laki-laki*	*abang*

car	*mobil*	*kereta*
city	*kota*	*bandar*
clever	*pintar*	*pandai*
cold (adj)	*dingin*	*sejuk*
cute (baby)	*lucu*	*manis*
delicious	*enak*	*sedap*
fetch someone	*menjemput*	*mengambil*
friend	*teman*	*kawan*
hour of the day	*jam …*	*pukul …*
to invite	*mengundang*	*menjemput*
marry	*menikah*	*kawin*
meet	*bertemu*	*berjumpa*
Mr (formal)	*Bapak*	*Tuan*
Mrs (formal)	*Ibu*	*Puan*
never	*tidak pernah*	*tak pernah*
office	*kantor*	*pejabat*
petrol	*bensin*	*petrol*
return	*kembali*	*balik*
room	*kamar*	*bilik*
shoes	*sepatu*	*kasut*
shop	*toko*	*kedai*
soon	*sebentar*	*sekejap*
speak	*berbicara*	*bercakap*
staff	*pegawai*	*kakitangan*
Sunday	*Hari Minggu*	*Hari Ahad*
toilet	*WC, kamar kecil*	*tandas*
understand	*mengerti*	*faham*
village	*desa*	*kampung*

Vocabulary

A

above – *diatas*
accident – *kecelakaan*
accompany – *menemani*
actually – *sebenarnya*
address – *alamat*
admit – *mengakui*
adult – *orang dewasa*
advice – *nasehat*
aerogram – *aerogram*
aeroplane – *pesawat udara*
afraid – *takut*
after – *sesudah*
afternoon – *siang/sore*
again – *lagi*
age – *umur*
agent – *agen*
ago – *yang lalu*
agree – *setuju*
agriculture – *pertanian*
airmail – *pos udara*
airport – *lapangan udara/ lapangan terbang*
alive – *hidup*
all – *semua*
allergic – *alergi*
alley – *gang*

already – *sudah*
also – *juga*
always – *selalu*
among – *diantara*
and – *dan*
angry – *marah*
animal – *binatang*
answer (v) – *jawab* (root word) *menjawab* (active verb)
ant – *semut*
antibiotics – *antibiotik*
anything – *apa saja*
anytime – *kapan saja*
anywhere – *dimana saja*
apple – *apel*
approximately – *kira-kira*
arm – *lengan*
arrive – *datang*
artist – *seniman*
ashamed – *malu*
ashtray – *asbak*
ask (v) – *tanya* (root word) – *bertanya* (active verb)
asleep – *tidur*
assist – *bantu* (root word) – *membantu* (active verb)

105

VOCABULARY

assistance – *bantuan*
at (location) – *di*
at (time) – *pada*

B

baby – *bayi*
babysitter – *penjaga anak*
bad (eg attitude) – *jahat*
bad (eg weather) – *buruk*
bad (eg thought) – *jelek*
bag – *tas*
baggage – *barang-barang*
ballpoint pen – *bolpoin*
banana – *pisang*
bank – *bank*
bank draft – *surat wesel*
bank clerk – *pegawai bank*
barber – *tukang cukur rambut*
bargain (v) – *tawar-menawar*
basket – *keranjang*
bathe – *mandi*
bathroom – *kamar mandi*
beach – *pantai*
beans – *buncis*
beautiful (scenery) – *indah*
beautiful (thing) – *bagus*
beautiful (woman) – *cantik*
because – *karena, sebab*
bed – *tempat tidur*
beef – *daging sapi*
beer – *bir*

before – *sebelum*
behind – *dibelakang*
better – *lebih baik*
between – *antara*
bicycle – *sepeda*
big – *besar*
bill (money) – *uang kertas*
bill – *bon, rekening*
bird – *burung*
black – *hitam*
blanket – *selimut*
bleed – *berdarah*
blood – *darah*
blue – *biru*
board (n) – *papan*
boat – *perahu*
boil – *merebus*
boiled egg – *telur rebus*
boiled water – *air matang*
bone – *tulang*
book – *buku*
bookshop – *toko buku*
border – *perbatasan*
bored – *bosan*
both – *keduanya/dua-duanya*
bottle – *botol*
bottle opener – *alat pembuka botol*
boy – *(anak) laki-laki*
brain – *otak*
branch (office) – *cabang*
bread – *roti*

break (things) – *pecah*

breakfast – *makan pagi*

breath – *napas*

bridge – *jembatan*

broken – *patah*

broom – *sapu*

brother (older) – *kakak laki-laki*

brother (younger) – *adik laki-laki*

brown – *coklat*

building – *gedung/bangunan*

burn – *bakar*

bus station – *stasiun, terminal bis*

bus – *bis*

businessperson – *pengusaha*

busy (location) – *ramai*

busy (time/schedule) – *sibuk*

but – *tetapi*

butter – *mentega*

buttons – *kancing*

buy – *beli* (root word) – *membeli* (active verb)

C

cabbage – *kol*

cabin – *ruang*

cake – *kue*

calm – *tenang*

camera – *kamera*

camp (v) – *kemah* (root word) – *berkemah* (active verb)

candle – *lilin*

can opener – *alat pembuka kaleng*

car – *mobil*

careful – *hati-hati*

cash – *uang tunai*

cat – *kucing*

cave – *gua/goa*

chair – *kursi*

change (v) – *ganti* (root word) – *mengganti* (active verb)

cheap – *murah*

chemist – *apotik*

cheque – *cek*

chicken – *ayam*

child – *anak*

children – *anak-anak*

chilli – *cabe*

chocolate – *coklat*

cholera – *kolera*

cigarettes – *rokok*

cinema – *bioskop*

city – *kota besar*

clean (adj) – *bersih*

clean (v) – *bersih* (root word) *membersihkan* (active verb)

clear, understood – *jelas*

climb (v) – *naik/mendaki*

closed – *tutup*
clothing – *pakaian*
cloudy – *mendung*
coconut – *kelapa*
coffee – *kopi*
coins – *uang logam*
cold (head) – *pilek/sakit selesma*
cold – *dingin*
colour – *warna*
comb – *sisir*
come – *datang*
commission – *komisi*
complain – *mengeluh*
complaint – *keluhan*
concert – *konser*
condom – *kondom*
confirmation – *penegasan*
constipation – *sukar buang air besar*
cook (v) – *masak*
cordial – *sirup*
corner – *sudut*
cost (object) – *harga*
cost (service) – *ongkos*
cough (v) – *batuk*
count – *hitung*
country – *negara*
cow – *sapi*
crab – *kepiting*
cremation – *pembakaran mayat*
crossroad – *perempatan*
crowded – *ramai*
cucumber – *ketimun*
cup – *cangkir*

D

dangerous – *bahaya*
dark – *gelap*
date – *tanggal*
daughter – *anak perempuan*
day – *hari*
day after tomorrow – *lusa*
deforestation – *penebangan hutan*
delicious – *enak*
dentist – *dokter gigi*
depart – *berangkat*
deposit (luggage) – *titip* (root word) – *menitipkan* (active verb)
develop (film) – *mencuci*
diarrhoea – *diare/mencret*
dictionary – *kamus*
different – *berbeda*
difficult – *sukar/susah*
dinner – *makan malam*
dirty – *kotor*
discount – *korting*
disease – *penyakit*

dive (v) – *selam* (root word)
    – *menyelam* (active
    verb)
do – *kerjakan*
doctor – *dokter*
dog – *anjing*
door – *pintu*
drink – *minum*
driver's licence – *SIM, Surat
  Ijin Mengemudi*
drop – *jatuh*
drug store – *toko obat*
dry (adj) – *kering*
dry (v) – *jemur* (root word)
    – *menjemur* (active
    verb)
duck – *bebek*
during – *selama*
dust – *debu*
duty – *tugas*
dysentery – *disentri*

E

each – *tiap-tiap*
ear – *telinga*
early – *pagi-pagi*
east – *timur*
easy – *mudah*
eat – *makan*
economy – *ekonomi*
educate – *mendidik*

education – *pendidikan*
egg – *telur*
electricity – *listrik*
embassy – *kedutaan*
emergency – *darurat*
empty (adj) – *kosong*
endorsement – *pengesahan*
engineer – *insinyur*
enough – *cukup*
enter – *masuk*
entrance – *jalan/pintu masuk*
envelope – *amplop*
essential – *perlu*
every – *masing-masing*
everybody – *semua orang*
everything – *segala sesuatu*
example – *contoh*
excuse – *alasan*
excuse me – *permisi*
expensive – *mahal*
experience – *pengalaman*
export (v) – *mengekspor*
eye – *mata*

F

face – *muka*
factory – *pabrik*
family – *keluarga*
fan – *kipas*
far – *jauh*
  Is it far? – *Jauh?*

farmer – *petani*
fast (adj) – *cepat*
fast (n, v) – *puasa*
father – *bapak, ayah*
female – *perempuan*
fever – *demam*
few – *beberapa*
film – *filem*
finger – *jari*
finished – *habis*
fish (n) – *ikan*
fish (v) – *memancing*
flashlight (torch) – *senter*
flour – *tepung*
flower – *bunga*
follow – *ikut*
food – *makanan*
food stall – *warung*
foot – *kaki*
for – *untuk/buat*
foreign – *asing*
foreigner – *orang asing*
forest – *hutan*
fork – *garpu*
fresh – *segar*
fried – *goreng*
friend – *teman*
frog – *kodok*
from – *dari*
front – *depan*
fruit – *buah-buahan*

G

game – *mainan*
garden – *kebun*
garlic – *bawang putih*
gentle – *lembut*
geography – *ilmu bumi*
giant – *raksasa*
gift – *hadiah*
girl – *perempuan*
give – *beri* (root word)
      – *memberi* (active verb)
glad – *senang*
glass – *gelas*
glasses (eye) – *kaca mata*
glue – *lem*
goat – *kambing*
gold – *emas*
good – *bagus*
goodbye (you are leaving) –
      selamat tinggal
goodbye (you are staying) –
      selamat jalan
government – *pemerintah*
grammar – *tatabahasa*
grape – *anggur*
grass – *rumput*
green – *hijau*
ground – *tanah*
group – *kelompok*
guest – *tamu*

H

habit – *kebiasaan*
hair – *rambut*
half – *setengah*
hand – *tangan*
handsome (male) – *tampan/ganteng*
happy – *gembira*
harbour – *pelabuhan*
hard – *keras*
hat – *topi*
head – *kepala*
headache – *sakit kepala*
health – *kesehatan*
hear – *dengar*
heart – *jantung*
heat – *kepanasan*
heavy – *berat*
help – *tolong*
here – *disini*
high – *tinggi*
hill – *bukit*
hire/rent – *sewa*
historical ruins – *runtuhan*
history – *sejarah*
hole – *lobang*
holiday – *liburan*
honest – *terus terang*
horn – *tanduk*
horse – *kuda*
hospital – *rumah sakit*

hot – *panas*
hot (spicy) – *pedas*
hour – *jam*
how – *bagaimana*
  How many? (animals) – *berapa ekor?*
  How many? (goods) – *berapa buah?*
  How much? – *berapa?*
humid – *lembab*
hungry – *lapar*
hunt (v) – *berburu*
husband – *suami*

I

I – *saya, aku*
  I'm Chris. – *Saya Chris.*
ice cream – *es krim*
ice – *es*
idea – *ide*
identification – *surat keterangan*
if – *kalau*
imagine – *membayangkan*
immediately – *dengan segera*
important – *penting*
  It's (not) important – *(Tidak) penting*
indigenous – *asli*
Indonesia – *Indonesia*
  I (don't) speak Indonesian. – *Saya tidak bisa bicara bahasa Indonesia.*
infection – *infeksi*
information – *keterangan*
injection – *suntikan*
insect – *serangga*
inside – *didalam*
insurance – *asuransi*
interesting – *menarik*
intersection – *persimpangan*
island – *pulau*
itch – *gatal*
ivory – *gading*

J

jacket – *jaket*
jackfruit – *nangka*
jail – *penjara*
jar – *toples*
jealous – *iri hati*
jewellery – *perhiasan*
job – *pekerjaan*
journalist – *wartawan*
jump (across) – *lompat*
jump (high) – *loncat*
just – *baru*
just one – *satu saja*
justice – *keadilan*

K

key – *kunci*
kiss – *cium* (root word) – *mencium* (active verb)
kitchen – *dapur*
knife – *pisau*
know (v) – *tahu*

L

lake – *danau*
lamb – *domba*
land – *tanah*

landscape – *pengaturan tanaman*
language – *bahasa*
last – *terakhir*
late – *terlambat*
later – *nanti*
laugh – *tertawa*
laundry – *binatu*
law – *hukum*
lawyer – *ahli hukum*
lay down – *berbaring*
leak – *bocor*
leather – *kulit*
lecture – *kuliah*
lecturer – *dosen*
left (opposite of right) – *kiri*
leg – *kaki*
lemon – *jeruk nipis*
length – *panjang*
letter – *surat*
lice – *kutu*
life – *hidup*
light (adj) – *ringan*
light (n) – *lampu*
like (v) – *suka*
little, a – *sedikit*
little (small) – *kecil*
live (exist/dwell) – *tinggal*
liver – *hati*
lock – *kunci*
long (measure) – *panjang*
long (time) – *lama*

look – *lihat*
loose – *longgar*
lose – *hilang*
lost – *kesasar*
lotion – *cairan*
lounge (room) – *ruang tamu*
love – *kasih, cinta, sayang*
   I love you. – *Saya sayang kamu.*
luck – *untung*
lunch – *makan siang*

M

mad – *gila*
magazine – *majalah*
main – *utama*
make (v) – *buat* (root word)
   – *membuat* (active verb)
malaria – *malaria*
male – *laki-laki*
man – *orang laki-laki*
mango – *mangga*
many – *banyak*
map – *peta*
marry – *menikah* (polite), *kawin*
market – *pasar*
mask – *topeng*
matches – *korek api*

material (for clothes) – *bahan baju*
mattress – *kasur*
may – *boleh*
meaning – *arti/makna*
  Waht does it mean? – *Apa artinya?*
meat – *daging*
medicine – *obat/obat-obatan*
meet – *bertemu*
menu – *daftar makanan*
message – *pesan*
milk – *susu*
mineral water – *Aqua, air soda*
minute – *menit*
mirror – *cermin/kaca*
Miss – *Nona*
mistake – *salah*
misunderstanding – *salah paham*
money – *uang*
monkey – *kera/monyet*
month – *bulan*
more – *lebih*
morning – *pagi*
Moslem – *orang Islam*
mosque – *mesjid*
mosquito – *nyamuk*
mosquito net – *kelambu*
most (the) – *(yang) paling*
mother – *ibu*
motorcycle – *sepeda motor*

mountain – *gunung*
movies – *bioskop*
Mr – *Bapak, Tuan*
Mrs – *Ibu, Nyonya*
much – *banyak*
mud – *lumpur*
museum – *musium*
music – *musik*
must – *harus*
mutton – *daging domba*

N

name – *nama*
  What is your name? – *Siapa nama saudara/anda?*
napkin – *serbet*
nationality – *kebangsaan*
near – *dekat*
Is it near here? – *Dekat dari sini?*
necessary – *perlu*
need – *perlu, butuh*
neighbour – *tetangga*
nervous – *gelisah*
never – *tidak pernah*
never mind – *tidak apa-apa*
new – *baru*
newspaper – *koran*
nice – *bagus*
night – *malam*
no, not – *tidak, bukan*

noisy – *ribut*
noodles – *mie*
north – *utara*
nose – *hidung*
not yet – *belum*
now – *sekarang*
nude – *telanjang*
number – *nomor*
nurse – *jururawat*
nut – *kacang*

O

object – *benda*
occupation – *pekerjaan*
ocean – *laut*
odd (number) – *ganjil*
odd (strange) – *aneh*
offer – *tawaran*
office – *kantor*
often – *sering*
old – *tua*
older brother – *abang*
older sister – *kakak*
once – *satu kali/sekali*
once again – *sekali lagi*
onion – *bawang bombay*
only – *hanya*
open – *buka*
operation – *operasi*
or – *atau*
orange – *jeruk manis*

over here – *disini*
over there – *disana*
owe – *berhutang*

P

pain – *sakit*
paintings – *lukisan*
paper – *kertas*
parcel – *paket, bungkusan*
park – *taman*
park (v) – *parkir*
pawpaw – *papaya*
pay (v) – *bayar* (root word)
  – *membayar* (active verb)
peanut – *kacang*
pen – *pena*
penalty – *hukuman*
pepper – *lada*
percent – *persen*
perhaps – *barangkali/mungkin*
person – *orang*
petrol – *bensin*
pharmacy – *apotik*
photograph – *foto*
picture – *gambar*
pig – *babi*
pillow – *bantal*
pineapple – *nanas, nenas*
place – *tempat*
plane – *pesawat terbang/udara*
plant (n) – *tanaman*

plate – *piring*
please – *silakan/tolong*
plus – *tambah*
poisonous – *beracun*
police – *polisi*
poor – *miskin*
pork – *daging babi*
possibly – *mungkin*
post office – *kantor pos*
postage – *perangko*
postcard – *kartu pos*
pot (cooking) – *panci*
potato – *kentang*
prefer (v) – *lebih suka*
pregnant – *hamil*
prescription – *resep*
problem – *masalah*
profession – *pekerjaan*
pull (v) – *tarik*
puppets – *wayang (kulit/golek)*
push – *dorong* (root word)
    – *mendorong* (active
            verb)

R

rain – *hujan*
razor – *alat cukur*
razor blade – *silet*
read – *membaca*
ready – *siap*
receipt – *kwitansi*
receive – *menerima*
red – *merah*
reforestation – *reboisasi*
refrigerator – *lemari es*
refuse (v) – *tolak* (root word)
        – *menolak* (active
                verb)
region – *wilayah*
religion – *agama*

Q

quality – *kwalitas*
quantity – *jumlah*
question – *pertanyaan*
quickly – *cepat*
quiet – *sepi/tenang*
quinine – *kina*

VOCABULARY

remember – *ingat*

rent (v) – *sewa* (root word)
 – *menyewa* (active verb)

repair – *memperbaiki*

repeat – *mengulangi*

reply (n) – *balasan/jawaban*

reply (v) – *membalas/menjawab*

request (v) – *minta, mohon*

reservation – *pesanan tempat*

respect – *hormat*

responsibility – *tanggung jawab*

restaurant – *rumah makan, restoran*

return – *kembali*

rheumatism – *encok*

rice (cooked) – *nasi*

rice (uncooked) – *beras*

rich – *kaya*

right (correct) – *benar*

right (opposite of left) – *kanan*

ring – *cincin*

ripe – *matang*

river – *sungai*

road – *jalan*

roasted – *panggang*

rock – *batu*

roof – *atap*

room – *kamar*

rope – *tali/tambang*

rotten – *busuk, rusak*

round – *bulat*

rubbish – *sampah*

run – *lari*

S

sail – *layar*

sailor – *pelaut*

salt – *garam*

salty – *asin*

same – *sama*

sand – *pasir*

sandals – *sandal*

scared – *takut*

scenery – *pemandangan*

school – *sekolah*

sea – *laut*

season – *musim*

seat – *tempat duduk*

seat belt – *sabuk pengaman*

second (unit of time) – *detik*

see – *lihat*

seldom – *jarang*

sell – *jual*

send (v) – *kirim* (root word)
 – *mengirim* (active verb)

sentence – *kalimat*

servant – *pembantu*

service – *pelayanan*

service charge – *ongkos*

sew – *jahit*
shade – *teduh*
shampoo (n) – *sampo*
shampoo (v) – *keramas*
shave – *cukur*
sheet (bed) – *seprei*
shells – *batok*
ship – *kapal*
shoelaces – *tali sepatu*
shop – *toko*
shrimp – *udang*
shut – *tutup*
sick – *sakit*
signature – *tandatangan*
silver – *perak*
since – *sejak*
singer – *penyanyi*
sister (older) – *kakak perempuan*
sister (younger) – *adik perempuan*
sit – *duduk*
skin – *kulit*
sleep – *tidur*
sleeping bag – *tas tidur*
slow – *pelan*
small – *kecil*
smell – *mencium*
snake – *ular*
soap – *sabun*
socks – *kaos kaki*
soft – *lembut*

some – *beberapa*
sometimes – *kadang-kadang*
son – *anak laki-laki*
song – *lagu*
sorry – *maaf*
sour – *asam*
south – *selatan*
soy sauce – *kecap asin*
speak – *bicara*
spicy – *pedas*
spoon – *sendok*
stairs – *tangga*
stale – *busuk*
stamp – *perangko*
starfruit – *belimbing*
stationmaster – *kepala stasiun*
stomach – *perut*
stomachache – *sakit perut*
stone – *batu*
stop! – *stop! berhenti!*
strange – *aneh*
street – *jalan*
student (school) – *pelajar*
student (university) – *mahasiswa*
style – *gaya*
sugar – *gula*
suitcase – *kopor*
sun – *matahari*
sunburnt – *kulit terbakar*
surface mail – *pos biasa*
sweet (adj) – *manis*

sweets – *permen*
swim (v) – *renang* (root word)
      – *berenang* (active
              verb)
swimsuit – *baju renang*

T

table – *meja*
tablet – *tablet*
tailor – *penjahit*
take off (depart) – *berangkat*
tampons – *tampon*
taste – *rasa*
tax – *pajak*
taxi – *taksi*
tea – *teh*
teacher – *guru*
teeth – *gigi*
telegram – *kawat*
telephone – *telpon*
television – *televisi*
teller – *kasir*
temple – *candi*
tent – *tenda*
thank you – *terima kasih*
that – *itu*
theatre (play) – *gedung
   sandiwara*
there is – *ada*
they – *mereka*
thirsty – *haus*

this – *ini*
thread – *benang*
throat – *tenggorokan*
ticket – *karcis*
ticket window – *loket*
tiger – *harimau*
tight – *sempit*
time: What time is it? – *Jam
   berapa?*
timetable – *daftar*
tired – *lelah*
to – *ke*
today – *hari ini*
together – *sama-sama*
toilet paper – *kertas kamar
   kecil*
toilet – *kamar kecil*
tomorrow – *besok*
tongue – *lidah*
too – *terlalu*
tool – *alat*
tooth – *gigi*
toothbrush – *sikat gigi*
torch (flashlight) – *senter*
touch – *sentuh*
tourist – *turis*
towel – *handuk*
traffic jam – *macet*
train – *kereta api*
travel (v) – *jalan-jalan*
travellers' cheque – *cek turis*
tree – *pohon*

VOCABULARY

truck – *trek, truk*
true – *benar*
turn – *belok*
typhoid – *demam tipus*

U

umbrella – *payung*
under – *dibawah*
understand (v) – *mengerti*
  I (don't) understand. –
  Saya (tidak) mengerti.
underwear – *pakaian dalam*
unemployment – *pengang-
  guran*
university – *universitas*
unripe – *mentah*

V

valley – *lembah*
vegetables – *sayur-sayuran*
very – *sangat*
village – *desa*
volcano – *gunung api*
vomit – *muntah*
vulgar – *kasar*

W

wait – *tunggu*
waiter – *pelayan*

wake up – *bangun*
walk – *jalan kaki*
wall – *dinding*
want (v) – *mau*
warm – *hangat*
wash – *cuci*
Watch out! – *Hati-hati!*
water – *air*
  boiled water – *air matang*
  purified water – *air putih*
waterfall – *air terjun*
watermelon – *semangka*
waves – *ombak*
we – *kami, kita* (see Grammar
  chapter, page 19)
weather – *cuaca*
week – *minggu*
weigh (v) – *imbang* (root word)
  menimbang (active verb)
welcome: You're welcome. –
  Kembali. Sama-sama
west – *barat*
wet – *basah*
what – *apa*
wheel – *roda*
What? – *Apa?*
  What is that? – *Apa itu?*
  What is your name? –
  Siapa nama saudara/anda?
  What time is it? – *Jam
  berapa sekarang?*
When? – *Kapan? Bilamana?*

Where? – *Di mana?*
which – *yang mana*
white – *putih*
Who? – *Siapa?*
  Who is calling? – *Siapa yang menelpon?*
whole – *penuh*
Why? – *Mengapa? Kenapa?*
wife – *istri*
wind – *angin*
window – *jendela*
wine – *anggur*
with – *dengan*
without – *tanpa*
woman – *orang perempuan/ wanita*
wood (timber) – *kayu*
woodcarving – *ukiran kayu*
wool – *wol*

word – *kata*
world – *dunia*
writer – *penulis*
writing paper – *kertas tulis*

Y

year – *tahun*
yellow – *kuning*
yes – *ya*
yesterday – *kemarin*
yield – *hasil*
you – *saudara, anda*
young – *muda*

Z

zoo – *kebun binatang*

Emergencies

Help!	*Tolong!*
It's an emergency!	*Keadaan darurat!*
There's been an accident!	*Ada kecelakaan!*
Call a doctor!	*Panggil dokter!*
Call an ambulance!	*Panggil ambulan!*
I've been robbed!	*Saya dirampok!*
Stop!	*Stop!*
Go away!	*Pergi!*
I'll get the police!	*Saya akan panggil polisi!*
Watch out!	*Awas!*
Thief!	*Copet!*
Fire!	*Kebakaran!*
I've lost ...	*Saya kehilangan ...*
my bag	*tas saya*
my money	*uang saya*
my travellers' cheque	*cek wisata saya*
my passport	*paspor saya*
I am ill.	*Saya sakit.*
I am lost.	*Saya kesasar.*
Where is the police station?	*Dimana ada kantor polisi?*
Where are the toilets?	*Dimana ada WC?*

Could you help me please?	*Boleh minta tolong?*
Could I please use the telephone?	*Boleh saya pakai telepon?*
I wish to contact my embassy/consulate.	*Saya mau menghubungi kedutaan besar/konsulat saya.*
I speak English.	*Saya berbahasa Inggris.*
I have medical insurance.	*Saya punya asuransi kesehatan.*
I understand.	*Saya mengerti.*
I don't understand.	*Saya tidak mengerti.*
I didn't realize that I was doing anything wrong.	*Saya tidak tahu kalau saya salah.*
I didn't do it.	*Saya tidak melakukan itu.*
I'm sorry. I apologise.	*Saya menyesal. Saya minta maaf.*
My contact number (next of kin)	*Nomor teleponsaya (saudara dekat)*
My blood group is ...	*Golongan darah saya ...*
(A, B, O, AB) positive/negative	*(A, B, O, AB) positif/negatif*

Index

LONELY PLANET PHRASEBOOKS

Complete your travel experience with a Lonely Planet phrasebook. Developed for the independent traveller, the phrasebooks enable you to communicate confidently in any practical situation – and get to know the local people and their culture.

Skipping lengthy details on where to get your drycleaning ironed, information in the phrasebooks covers bargaining, customs and protocol, how to address people and introduce yourself, explanations of local ways of telling the time, dealing with bureaucracy and bargaining, plus plenty of ways to share your interests and learn from locals.

Arabic (Egyptian)
Arabic (Moroccan)
Australian
*Introduction to Australian English,
Aboriginal and Torres Strait languages.*
Baltic States
*Covers Estonian, Latvian and
Lithuanian.*
Bengali
Brazilian
Burmese
Cantonese
Central Europe
*Covers Czech, French, German,
Hungarian, Italian and Slovak.*
Eastern Europe
*Covers Bulgarian, Czech, Hungarian,
Polish, Romanian and Slovak.*
Ethiopian (Amharic)
Fijian
Greek
Hindi/Urdu
Indonesian
Japanese
Korean
Lao
Latin American (Spanish)
Mandarin

Mediterranean Europe
*Covers Albanian, Greek, Italian,
Macedonian, Maltese, Serbian &
Croatian and Slovene.*
Mongolian
Nepali
Papua New Guinea (Pidgin)
Pilipino
Quechua
Russian
Scandinavian Europe
*Covers Danish, Finnish, Icelandic,
Norwegian and Swedish.*
Sri Lanka
Swahili
Thai
Thai Hill Tribes
Tibetan
Turkish
USA
*Introduction to US English,
Vernacular Talk, Native American
languages and Hawaiian.*
Vietnamese
Western Europe
*Useful words and phrases in Basque,
Catalan, Dutch, French, German, Irish,
Portuguese and Spanish (Castilian).*

LONELY PLANET AUDIO PACKS

Audio packs are an innovative combination of a cassette/CD and phrasebook presented in an attractive cloth wallet made from indigenous textiles by local communities.

The cassette/CD presents each language in an interactive format. A number of successful language teaching techniques are used, enabling listeners to remember useful words and phrases with little effort and in an enjoyable way.

Travellers will learn essential words and phrases – and their correct pronunciation – by participating in a realistic story. The scripts have been developed in the belief that the best way to learn a new language is to hear it, then to practise it in the context in which you will use it. The emphasis is on effective communication.

The cassette/CD complements the relevant phrasebook, and the cloth wallet makes the pack an attractive and convenient package – easy to display in shops and useful and practical for travellers.

Cassettes & CDs
- complement phrasebooks
- realistic storylines explore situations that will be useful for all travellers
- languages are spoken by native speakers
- listeners learn key words and phrases in repetition exercises, then hear them used in context
- realistic sound effects and indigenous music used throughout
- length: 80 minutes

Cloth Pack
- ticket-wallet size – suitable for airline tickets, notes etc
- made from traditional textiles woven and sewn by local communities
- cardboard reinforced and sealed in plastic for easy display
- size: 140 x 260 mm

Available now: Indonesian audio pack; Japanese audio pack; Thai audio pack

PLANET TALK

Lonely Planet's FREE quarterly newsletter

Every issue is packed with up-to-date travel news
and advice including:

- a letter from Lonely Planet co-founders Tony and
  Maureen Wheeler
- go behind the scenes on the road with a Lonely
  Planet author
- feature article on an important and topical travel
  issue
- a selection of recent letters from travellers
- details on forthcoming Lonely planet promotions
- complete list of Lonely Planet products

To join our mailing list contact any Lonely Planet office.

LONELY PLANET PUBLICATIONS

AUSTRALIA
PO Box 617, Hawthorn 3122, Victoria
tel: (03) 9819 1877 fax: (03) 9819 6459
e-mail: talk2us@lonelyplanet.com.au

USA
Embarcadero West,
155 Filbert St, Suite 251,
Oakland, CA 94607
tel: (510) 893 8555
TOLL FREE: 800 275-8555
fax: (510) 893 8563
e-mail: info@lonelyplanet.com

UK
10 Barley Mow Passage, Chiswick,
London W4 4PH
tel: (0181) 742 3161 fax: (0181) 742 2772
e-mail: 100413.3551@compuserve.com

FRANCE:
71 bis rue du Cardinal Lemoine, 75005
Paris
tel: 1 44 32 06 20 fax: 1 46 34 72 55
e-mail: 100560.415@compuserve.com

World Wide Web: http://www.lonelyplanet.com